FINDING OUR SEA-LEGS

FINDING OUR SEA-LEGS

ETHICS, EXPERIENCE AND THE OCEAN OF STORIES

WILL BUCKINGHAM

First edition published by Kingston University Press, 2009.
Revised and updated edition published by Wind&Bones, 2019.

Contents © Will Buckingham 2009 & 2019

Published by Wind&Bones 2019
www.windandbones.com

ISBN: 978-1-9993764-0-6

Typeset with Vellum

Cover image: *Wind-tossed Seas at Shichiri Beach in Sagami Province*
Utagawa Hiroshige (1852). Public Domain.
Courtesy of LACMA. www.lacma.org

Cover design © Will Buckingham 2019

For my parents,
and for storytellers everywhere...

CONTENTS

PREFACE TO THE UPDATED EDITION

As the Canadian poet, Erin Mouré once said, books are emigrants: they belong where they end up. It is ten years since *Finding Our Sea-Legs* cast off from its moorings, thanks to the navigational skill of Kingston University Press. When I first launched this book, it was my hope that it might at least prove to be seaworthy, and that it might stand the test of time—or at the very least, that it might not sink the moment it left port. Back then, as it listed towards the horizon, I was under no illusions about what a deeply peculiar thing it was. This bundle of tales of talking fish, drunken Indonesian gods and philosophical woodpeckers didn't look much like the sleek philosophical craft that plied the waters of academic philosophy. It had none of their clean, aerodynamic lines. It was more cobbled-together than it was engineered. But the ramshackle construction of the book was not just accidental, a simple oversight on my own part; it was also essential to my own philosophical project. I see more clearly now in retrospect that the exuberance of the storytelling in the book was a revolt against philosophical boringness. The refusal to separate out from each other things that should properly be kept apart was a part of my hunch that, in experience, things do not come in tidy compartments. And the light-heartedness of tone, the love of digression and the frequent jokes were a protest against high seriousness as a way of seeing and understanding the world.

Over the past decade, *Sea-Legs* has continued to find its way into the hands of readers (*who are they?*). From time to time it has found itself on academic reading lists. It has had a particular appeal, it seems, to sceptical not-quite-Buddhist readers. And after ten years— like one of those clapped-out and apparently unseaworthy vessels that makes you ask *how can it still be afloat?*—it still seems somehow to be holding up. So—after a decade of quiet, modest journeys— this seems a good time to reissue the text in a new, revised edition.

For this second edition, I have as much as possible resisted the temptation to tinker with the text. I have corrected a number of glaring and sometimes embarrassing errors and made a number of small tweaks for style. Otherwise, as I remain broadly in agreement with the arguments set out here, I have left the main body of the text as it was when first published ten years ago. I have, however, added a brief afterword, which gives an idea of where I stand now; still nowhere near sight of solid ground.

The first edition never made it into an ebook edition. I have taken the opportunity to rectify this, and the book is now available both in reissued paperback and in all major ebook formats.

It is also, perhaps, worth mentioning the convention I have adopted in this new edition for diacritical marks when drawing upon resources from other traditions. In the original version of this book, I kept what is now the standard Romanised spelling for terms such as 'Buddha' and 'nirvana' that are more or less accepted parts of the standard lexicon, but when it came to less familiar terms, I preserved the diacritics. In this revised edition, at the risk of offending the purists, I have gone back on my earlier intention and removed the diacritics.

Otherwise, things are more or less where they stood a decade ago.

PREFACE

This book is an attempt to use the resources of both philosophy and storytelling to throw some light on how it might be possible to think through ethics. The argument of the book— or, at the very least, the story that I am telling—is one that cuts between texts, traditions and cultures. This is, in part, a necessary consequence of the subject-matter. Stories are by nature unruly beasts. Robert Irwin writes, in his perceptive study of the *Arabian Nights*, that good stories pay little attention to frontiers, whether these be cultural or linguistic (Irwin 1995). Because of this tendency of stories to go beyond the limits that many might think proper, as the book progresses, I will be moving freely between the rainforests of Papua New Guinea, twelfth century Kashmiri scriptures written entirely in the form of stories, fish that prophesy in Hebrew in the fish-markets of New York and the abstruse philosophical reflections of the likes of Immanuel Kant and Edmund Husserl. Such a method is suggested, if not dictated, by the demands of storytelling itself.

This is not a book that attempts to put forward a theory of ethics, a set of principles or rules by which we might know what is to be done and what is to be avoided. Instead, it is an attempt to move towards a deeper attentiveness to ethical *experience*. Ethics, in this view, is not only a matter of reflection from the comfort of one's armchair, but rather a living responsiveness to the demands, responsibilities and possibilities that are presented to us, moment by moment, as we go about our lives.

The book begins by using storytelling as a way of looking at the experience of ethics, and introduces the idea first put forward by Aristotle—that ethics is like navigation, that is to say, that ethics is not so much about finding a point of absolute certainty, as it is a matter of finding our way through the many uncertainties and perplexities of our existence. Chapter two then draws upon parables and stories from both East and West to suggest, philosophy having failed to deliver us to a safe harbour, that without taking leave of philosophy altogether, storytelling may provide a way of thinking that can help us better understand the wind and the tides. The third chapter then casts off upon the sea of stories with two tales—a story from the southern reaches of Papua New Guinea, and a Roma tale—to explore what kind of thinking goes on in the relating of stories. This question is explored further in chapter four with the help of Walter Benjamin and Franz Rosenzweig's reflections upon storytelling and experience. Stories, it will become apparent, are not only reflections upon experience, but they are themselves also experiences; and in this way they can act as a kind of phenomenology, a reflection upon appearances, upon the way that that world seems to manifest itself to us. Chapter five then considers the powerful stories that are told about ethics by the philosopher and phenomenologist Emmanuel Levinas. In this chapter, the philosophical waters are perhaps a little more treacherous than elsewhere, and so here we will have to move with some care and with a degree of patience. However, Levinas's work, for all its difficulty, will provide us with three things that we need to proceed smoothly on our way: firstly, the suggestion that ethical reflection needs a closer attention to experience itself; secondly, the insight that ethics is bound up with our nature as temporal beings, as beings who are born, who live and who all eventually die; and thirdly, the idea that ethics concerns our relationships with otherness, with the different kinds of difference that we encounter in the world. These three thoughts will then be recast in the three chapters that follow, using storytelling as a kind of phenomenological method. Chapter six explores what kind of a phenomenological method storytelling might be, by means of telling stories about the telling of stories. In chapter seven, this method is put to further use through telling tales that throw light on the curious fluidity and complexity of the times and spaces of experience in general, and of ethical experience in particular. Chapter eight then explores questions of otherness and difference, by means of tales of desert crossings, of talking fish and of sages from both East and West. The last chapter puts this all together to ask how it might be possible to attend more deeply to ethics once we have put all dreams of certainty and dry land to one side.

It was the philosopher Isaiah Berlin (1999) who famously divided thinkers and writers—be they storytellers or theorists —into hedgehogs, who know one big thing, and foxes, who know many things. I always stand in admiration of hedgehogs, but I am a fox by nature, and I want to preserve a fox-like ability to move light-footed between different kinds of knowledge. It is a general rule that hedgehogs like to write for hedgehogs, and foxes like to write for foxes. I am no different in this respect, and so I have decided to consign certain of the more technical philosophical arguments and clarifications to the footnotes rather than including them in the main body of the text. Here, in the notes, while the foxes are long disappeared over the hill, following their noses and incapable of sticking to one thing, the hedgehogs may find at least something to satisfy them.

IN THE MARKETPLACE IN DARJEELING, EARLY ONE MORNING

We left the hotel in Darjeeling early, shouldering our bags and heading through the narrow streets to the bazaar where the jeep was waiting. The air was still a little chilly and the sun was low over the hills, but already the marketplace was crowded. As we hurried through the crowds, we heard the sound of wailing. There, to the side of the road by a flight of steps, was a man. He was seated on the ground amid the detritus of the market, sniffed at by mangy dogs. Nobody was paying him any attention. His clothes had slipped away from his upper body to reveal a hollow chest. His ribs stood out starkly in relief. Skinny arms protruded from his rags; he hugged himself with one arm while propping himself up with the other. But it was not his emaciated form that shocked me most. Instead, it was his face that I remember, an abyss of distress and misery. We faltered for a moment as he cried out, his face contorted in pain.

What would it have taken to have alleviated his suffering? Perhaps a universe, perhaps merely the touch of another human being's hands. Or perhaps he was beyond helping, if there is such a thing as being beyond helping. But we were tired and ready for our journey to end. This man was a stranger, not our concern. So we turned away from his suffering. After all, suffering is—as certain Indian texts maintain—as inexhaustible as the ocean;[1] and often it seems that there is little, so very little, that we can do. Inevitably, there are times when we no longer try. In a moment—just long enough for the thought 'there is nothing that we can do' to take root in our minds—we had turned away.

The crowds closed behind us, and the man was gone. We headed down the hill to where the jeep was waiting, unloaded our heavy bags, climbed in, and before long we were on our way down the winding road that led to Siliguri, speeding past signs reading 'Arrive home in peace, not in pieces (Public Works Dept.),' and, 'Don't test your nerves on my curves.'

Only then, with Darjeeling behind us, as we wound our way down towards the River Teesta, did my friend speak.

'We should have done something,' she said.

Philosophy, Ethics and Stories

Over a decade on, the memory of that morning still stays with me. *We should have done something.* There is no getting around it, no way of easily evading this thought. And asking, *Ah, yes, but what?*, admitting that we knew nothing of his suffering and that we simply do not know how much we could have done, does nothing to absolve me of this sense of responsibility. When it comes down to it, it is quite simple: we knew enough to act, but we failed to do so.

I begin with this story because for me it says something about the perplexity that lies at the heart of our attempts to think through ethics. And if ethics has been the abiding obsession of philosophers since the very beginning, it is in part because these kind of perplexing experiences are so very far from being uncommon. Often we find ourselves, our world and our values put into question in this way. Yet—and this is worth saying at the outset—frequently philosophy alone seems inadequate as a means of understanding such experiences. The philosophical language of rights and duties and consequences and virtues, a language that sometimes seems so necessary, is also one that often seems only obliquely related to actual ethical *experience*, to events such as those that took place in the marketplace in Darjeeling. Indeed, the moment that we confront urgent ethical questions in our everyday lives (or the moment these questions confront us) it often seems as if the abstractions provided by the philosophers are curiously illadapted to deal with them. This is the case, not least because—given that we live forwards, as Kierkegaard pointed out, but we reflect backwards[2]—the entire labour of philosophical ethics often seems to aim at a single judgement of acts that are already in the past: good or bad, yea or nay, condemn or commend.

And so, when thinking through with questions of ethics—by which I mean questions concerning how we relate to others and how we might be able to best conduct ourselves—even philosophers sometimes find themselves going beyond the precincts of philosophy proper. And when they do, it is often to stories that they turn.

Why stories? One reason is that, as Aristotle knew, when it comes to our activity in the world we are always dealing with particular circumstances rather than with generalities. He writes in the *Nicomachean Ethics*: 'matters concerned with conduct and questions of what is good for us have no fixity.' In the absence of such fixity, it is not so much a matter of subsuming particular circumstances under 'any art or set of precepts,' but rather, 'the agents themselves must in each case consider what is appropriate to the occasion, as happens also in the art of medicine or of navigation' (*Ethics* 1104a). That is to say, the world of ethics is not a world of pure abstraction, of eternal and immutable realities; instead it is this very world, where we find ourselves stumbling through the marketplace confronted first by this, then by that, where our knowledge is always partial and never absolute, where we never have enough time on our hands to come to a fully reasoned judgement, where the demands upon us always outstrip our ability to respond and we never fully know what the consequences of our actions will be. We grope our way towards understanding through the heart of uncertainty, and at no point can we be granted the luxury of being certain we are right, or discover the luxury of a rule that can deliver absolute results. Aristotle seems to be suggesting that, when it comes to conduct, we need a form of wisdom that allows us to act *amid* uncertainty, amid the jostling of the marketplace. And so, when I say that I do not know what I could have done to help the man in the bazaar in Darjeeling, this is not to divest myself of all responsibility; it is instead a straightforward admission of the uncertainty that makes this a situation that demands ethical reflection in the first place.

The Aristotelian idea that ethics is like navigation also suggests to us why it might be that stories are particularly well suited for the discussion of ethics. Stories, after all, do not deliver us certain truths in the form of propositions. They do not tell us unambiguously what is and what is not the case. More frequently than not, they do not so much do away with questions as multiply them. They do not deliver us to solid ground, but instead bring us face to face with the particularity, the uncertainty and liquidity of our existence. If ethics is a kind of navigation, then the territory upon which ethics is played out could be likened to a turbulent sea upon which, as one Buddhist text has it, beings bob and sink,[3] their troubles endless. And if we are to learn to be good or at least passable navigators, avoiding the most treacherous reefs, it may be that we cannot do without stories.

The Trouble With Ethics

Stories, however, are troubling things; and the suggestion that we might usefully think through ethics by means of stories might seem to risk introducing all kinds of further uncertainties into what is already a clouded and confused business. For many philosophers, uncertainty has been seen as the enemy of ethics. *If I cannot be certain what is right,* the question is, *how can I do the right thing?* And if this is a problem, perhaps there is scant comfort to be drawn from the fact that this has been a problem ever since the days of Socrates.

In Plato's dialogue, the *Euthyphro* the Athenian philosopher, gadfly and trouble-maker Socrates is outside the law-courts of Athens, where he is being indicted under charges of impiety. Outside the courts, he meets with a fervent young man called Euthyphro, who is prosecuting his father on similar grounds. It appears his father was responsible for the death of a slave, and Euthyphro wishes to call him to account. While modern readers might side with Euthyphro, in ancient Greece the idea of taking one's father to court, however high-minded the motives, was a deeply troubling one. So Socrates and Euthyphro fall into conversation about the nature of impiety. After all, this is something that concerns them both intimately, and for Socrates clearing up the question of what impiety actually *is* might well be a matter of life and death.

Some way into their discussion, Socrates lays out the problem.

SOCRATES: What are the subjects of difference that cause hatred and anger? Let us look at it this way. If you and I were to differ about numbers as to which is the greater, would this difference make us enemies and angry with each other, or would we proceed to count and soon resolve our difference about this?

EUTHYPHRO: We would certainly do so.

SOCRATES: Again, if we differed about the larger and the smaller, we would turn to measurement and soon cease to differ.

EUTHYPHRO: That is so.

SOCRATES: And about the heavier and the lighter, we would resort to weighing and be reconciled.

EUTHYPHRO: Of course.

SOCRATES: What subject of difference would make us angry and hostile to each other if we were unable to come to a decision? Perhaps you do not have an answer ready, but examine as I tell you whether these subjects are the just and the unjust, the beautiful and the ugly, the good and the bad. Are these not the subjects of difference about which, when we are unable to come to a satisfactory decision, you and I and other men become hostile to each other whenever we do? (*Euthyphro* 7b-d)

The problem is clear: there is no yardstick by virtue of which we can agree on right and wrong, good and bad. It is not just that we have not yet reached common agreement in ethics, but that we don't even know the method we might use to get there. This problem is about as far from being an abstract philosophical problem as is possible. As Socrates makes clear, it is precisely when it comes to questions of ethics—questions of good and bad, just and unjust—that we find ourselves becoming angry and hostile to each other. These are the things that get us hot under the collar. Whether for better or worse, it seems that we care passionately about ethics. We are impossibly and irredeemably social creatures who love and hate, who snuggle and struggle, who build friendships and enmities, for whom not caring is not an option, even when we know that our caring is inconsistent and without foundation. But at the same time, we have no common measure by virtue of which we could come to an ethical conclusion. If we happened to care passionately about the disputed molecular structure of some particular compound, we would hardly go to war over such a dispute, because we could resolve our differences by measuring or testing. But we do not have this advantage when it comes to ethics; and so, in the absence of this common measure, we face a situation of real and profound danger. Despite our best intentions—perhaps *because* of our best intentions—it is the conflicts between our ethical stances that are the major causes of human strife. Wars almost everywhere, even those we might judge to be the most profoundly unjust, are not launched on a whim, but on account of (real or imagined) harms and slights done to the party in question, or in pursuit of lofty dreams of a better world. Those who abuse make the ethical claim that those whom they abuse deserve this treatment. Everywhere there is human cruelty, everywhere there is barbarity, everywhere there is conflict, right at the heart of things you will find clamorous claims to ethical certainty, to truth, to right, to justice. We are accustomed, in short, to thinking of ethics as the solution; but it is also a large part of the problem. First we hear the ethical claims and counter-claims; next we hear the distant rumble of guns and the clanking of the ironsmiths' hammers as they fashion ploughshares into swords.

What, then, are we to do? At the end of the dialogue with Euthyphro, the young man confesses that he is baffled when it comes to a true understanding of the nature of piety and impiety. Socrates admits that he too is ignorant, and urges Euthyphro to keep on searching. With this, the two men part.

Under the circumstances, Socrates' advice to Euthyphro is not unreasonable. And yet, given that two and a half thousand years of searching have not delivered us the kinds of ethical certainties of which Socrates dreamed, it is also not unreasonable to wonder whether we might do better to take a rather different tack.

Navigating Ethics

Throughout the history of ethical thought, at least in the West, there have been repeated attempts to attain the kind of ethical certainty that might be able to meet Socrates's challenge head-on; and yet, to date, it seems that all have been unsuccessful. Certainly, many have *proclaimed* themselves successful; but to meet Socrates's criterion for success, it would be necessary not only to believe that one had attained this certainty, but also to establish a common measure that could be shared, so that we could mutually come to an eventual agreement. And this has never happened.

However, this is not sufficient reason for gloomy despair. After all, there may be something fearful lurking in the idea of moral certainty. When Immanuel Kant tells us that masturbation, selling one's hair to wig-makers and lying are always blameable acts,[4] we might want to protest that these things are not always worthy of such harsh judgements. Indeed we may want to hold out the possibility that there may be circumstances in which it is positively a good thing to do any or all of these things, although not, perhaps, all at the same time. Ethics, if it is to avoid becoming monstrous ('Herr Kant, do you have the man that I desire to murder hiding in your house?' 'Indeed I do, Sir, for I cannot tell a lie'[5]) simply *must* pay attention to the particular.

Let us return to Aristotle. If, when it comes to ethics, what matters is a closer attention to the particular circumstances in which we find ourselves, and if there is no fixity to be found in ethical matters, then it may be that this search for an immutable common foundation for ethics is *bound* to fail. And even if Aristotle is wrong, we have not yet reached this point: two and a half thousand years after Socrates, there is still no ethical agreement that would meet his exacting standards. Even if such agreement is not impossible *in principle* (although I suspect that it is), prolonging the search for such agreement may not be particularly useful *in practice*. We do not have the Socratic luxury of simply confessing our own ignorance and then continuing on our way. We have to act, and we find ourselves having to account for our actions.

How, then, are we to navigate through these perplexities and uncertainties? What can we use to guide us, while we are at the mercy of the wind and the tides, our circumstances changing moment by moment? The philosophers may shudder, but most of us know that we simply have to act as best we are able, through what scant knowledge we can pick up, through hunches and intuitions and everyday know-how, and through a good dose of the luck that (as the ancient Greeks had the wisdom to recognise) plays a far greater role in ethics than we are comfortable to admit. At first glance, this feels like a disavowal of the challenge set by Socrates. It may, however, be almost the opposite. If we cannot ease our tendency towards hostility and mutual enmity by reaching agreement, perhaps we can go some way to alleviating this tendency by a frank admission that, when we talk about ethics, none of us stands on anything like solid ground. When we talk about ethics, perhaps we are all—all of us, all of the time—all at sea.

2

ALL AT SEA: A PHILOSOPHICAL PARABLE

The story begins with a dream of solid ground: like the dream of a sailor who has been a long time at sea and who feels a longing for the hard, unmoving rocks beneath his feet. Having lived his entire life on board ship, and knowing only the swell of the ocean, our sailor nevertheless still feels some kind of longing; from time to time, when he looks towards the shimmer of the horizon, he imagines cliffs, mountains, sandy beaches, low forests, atolls, islands and continents. How beautiful the dream is. Yet the dreaming sailor turns away from the horizon with a sigh. He knows that his imagination is lurid, and that the haze and the heat of the noonday sun are playing tricks upon him, that he does not have the courage of his convictions. He has read the history books. He has studied the ship's log. He has striven to learn as much as he can. And although the dream still moves him, he is no longer courageous or foolish enough to dream it with the conviction he once had.

Our sailor is not alone on the ship. With him there are many others, and amongst this motley bunch are some—we can call them philosophers, prophets or priests, it does not matter which—who do not share his diffidence and his uncertainty. These prophets are a forbidding crowd: confident in their powers, they have clarified their vision by the force of long and difficult asceticism, disciplines of the body and of the soul and of the mind (although, alas, all too rarely of the heart). Most of the time, they sit in silence, cloistered in their cabins where they are not seen from one year to the next, locked in arcane conference in the canteen, or sitting on deck-chairs, staring at the unending sky and the roiling waves with looks of otherworldly puzzlement upon their faces. Most of the time, that is. For, on occasion, one amongst these curious prophets happens to lean over the guard-rail and glimpse (or claim to do so) a dark smudge where the sky meets the sea. *Land Ahoy!*[1]

Suddenly there is commotion. Some rush to the prophet's side muttering, 'Yes, yes! I see it! I see it!' Others, more cautious, remove their spectacles, draw out a cloth to clean the lenses, return the spectacles to their noses, and squint uncertainly in the direction of the pointed finger. Inevitably, from certain deckchairs that are positioned so that they might be perpetually in the shade, it is possible to hear dissenting voices, protests muttered between teeth clenched around the stem of a pipe: 'Bunkum!' the killjoys mutter.

For our sailor, these two simple words—*Land Ahoy!*—never fail to bring tears to his eyes. How wonderful, he thinks, if it were true. But he is under no illusions. He has seen it all before. Sometimes the prophet is all but ignored, despite the shouting, and they skulk off to brood in their cabin or deckchair. Sometimes the prophet receives a few polite smiles, nothing more ('Ah,' people mutter, 'another one!'). Sometimes the prophet gathers together a few followers who jump up and down, an enthusiastic and clamorous band. And although it has not happened in the sailor's own lifetime, in the ship's log it is recorded that, on several occasions in the past, a prophet afflicted by noontide delirium has gained enough support to seize the vessel. On occasions such as these, the ship's course has veered wildly and erratically for days, months, years even, as the increasingly fractious mutineers—for this is what they have become—point it first this way and then that, heading towards the dream of a port that was always out of reach. Yet for one reason or another, none of these prophets has ever succeeded in bringing the ship into a safe harbour. On the horizon, the dark smudges have perpetually receded into nothing at the approach of the boat; or they have vanished in the darkness of the night and failed to reappear in the dawn; or the prophet who has spoken so eloquently has disappeared overboard, never to be seen again.

How strange that we are still adrift. After all this time.

A Gnat's Fart

Western philosophy could be seen as one long dream of solid ground and of safe harbour. As the ship of philosophy has lurched across the oceans through the centuries—or perhaps it would be better to imagine a whole fleet of ships, with the attendant mutinies and piratical battles and exchanges of cannon fire, sinkings and drownings—this has been the most cherished, most fevered of the dreams that we have allowed ourselves to dream: that somewhere, just beyond the horizon, there might lie some solid ground. Yet nobody, to my knowledge, has found such a place. And if they have, they have never returned to tell us.[2]

That is not to say that two and a half thousand years of philosophical meditation have been in vain; it is only to say that the insights and results of philosophy have not yet saved us from the high seas where we all live and where we all, inevitably, must die. Because of this failure, it is easy to accuse philosophers of heady abstraction—like Socrates in Aristophanes's play, *The Clouds*, bobbing around in his curious sky-

borne gondola, without his feet ever touching the ground, speculating about the physiology of gnat farts and the jumping of
fleas.[3]

And so, we might find ourselves wondering: what *is* philosophy good for? Nautical engineering is good for building boats,
meteorology is good for predicting the movements of the
elements, medical knowledge is good for curing ailments of the
body, but *philosophy*? Some philosophers have claimed that
philosophy leads to certainty, but even the most learned of
them tend to disagree amongst themselves about the certainties to which philosophy has led them. Others have claimed
that philosophical knowledge is good for curing ailments of the
soul, but when one takes a good look not so much at philosophy as at *philosophers*, this seems implausible. Philosophers
may be no more sick-of-soul than the rest of us, but at the very
least they seem to be no more cured: for every philosopher who
seems well-balanced and—dare it be said?—*happy*, one can
cite the example of another who is frenzied, deranged, or in
one way or another unhinged.

Or perhaps we could see philosophers as storytellers. As
dreamers of strange and beautiful dreams. Or as gadflies, as
provokers of impossible questions that we had—until they
turned up with their quizzical glances—never even dreamed of
asking. Or as inventors of new ideas that allow us to think
about the world afresh. And the dreaming of strange and beautiful dreams, the asking of impossible questions and the invention of fresh ideas—all these amount to rather more than a
gnat's fart. Strange dreams may alert us once again to the
strange and dreamlike nature of our experience of the world, to
the astonishment and wonder of being here at all. Impossible
questions can often cast new light upon the world, can lead our
thoughts beyond their habitual circularity. And when the old
ideas fail to get us where we would like to be, perhaps new ones
may have the power to move us. None of this has anything to do

with certainty, but it may give rise to the kinds of insights that we need to help us along our way.

For many of those who are not philosophers, such philosophical dreams of dry land seem neither particularly compelling nor particularly urgent. We live, most of us, day-to-day. We do as best we can, putting up with the kind of things that would drive philosophers to distraction. We get on with the business of living, our approach to ethics both slapdash and *ad hoc*, a philosopher's nightmare, a hodge-podge of reasoning and impulse and stories and fragments of stories, knowledge drawn from here and there. Most of us, if we are not philosophers—and even those of us who are philosophers, when we are off-duty or off-guard—do not govern our lives by means of well-grounded rational principles. Instead, we make our way uneasily, attentive to the winds and the tides, our thoughts inconsistent and jumbled, with little clarity and even less certainty. And, astonishingly enough for the moralists, we often find that this kind of approach to going about our lives is remarkably successful in bringing about conditions whereby kindness and compassion can flourish. Confused though we are, we get by, in the main.

However, by renouncing dreams of dry land, and admitting that if philosophy has not managed to resolve the questions that trouble us, it is possible to see that philosophy may still have a role in giving us the kinds of know-how that we need as we go about this tricky business of navigating our way through our lives. The sages may be misguided in promising to deliver us to a safe harbour, but they may nevertheless help us to ride out the elements, to find ways of living as best we are able when the ground beneath our feet is always shifting and when we never know where the tides and the winds are going to deliver us next. Through the questions that we hadn't thought to ask, through the ideas that we hadn't known how to formulate, and through the dreams that we hadn't known how to dream, philosophy may enrich and deepen our sense of our situation, thereby easing the turbulence of our passage through the world. And if this is a less elevated goal than that dreamed of by our prophets, it is also arguably of more immediate and urgent importance.

A Sea of Stories

It is here that we see why, in our day to day lives, when we find ourselves talking about questions of ethics, we inevitably resort to the telling of stories, the spinning of yarns. Because if ethics is like navigation, then stories are like the sea. The latter simile may be less familiar than the former. It appears in the title of Somadeva's delightful collection of folk-tales, the *Kathasarit-sagara,* or 'Ocean of the Sea of Stories' (Somadeva, 1996), and recurs in the work of Salman Rushdie, who conjures up the image of this ocean with a storyteller's flair.

> So Iff the Water Genie told Haroun about the Ocean of the Streams of Story, and even though he was full of a sense of hopelessness and failure, the magic of the Ocean began to have an effect on Haroun. He looked into the water and saw that it was made up of a thousand thousand thousand and one different currents, each one a different colour, weaving in and out of one another like a liquid tapestry of breathtaking complexity; and Iff explained that these were the Streams of Story, that each coloured strand represented and contained a single tale. Different parts of the Ocean contained different sorts of stories, and as all the stories that had ever been told and many that were still in the process of being invented could be found here, the Ocean of the Streams of Story was in fact the biggest library in the universe. And because the stories were held here in fluid form, they retained the ability to change, to become new versions of themselves, to join up

with other stories and so become yet other stories; so that unlike a library of books, the Ocean of the Streams of Story was much more than a storeroom of yarns. It was not dead but alive. (Rushdie 1990, 71)

Rushdie perfectly captures the fluidity and mutability of stories, the way that—as Robert Irwin writes—tales 'evolve into other tales' and 'replicate, elaborate, invert, abridge, link and comment on their own structure in an endless play of transformation', so that in the end we find ourselves 'adrift on an endless ocean of stories, an ocean that is boundless, deep and ceaselessly in motion' (Irwin 1995, 65). This is a metaphor that is by no means found exclusively within Indian thought. It also recurs in the literature of the West, as has been pointed out by Ernst Curtius in his monumental *European Literature and the Latin Middle Ages*, where he dedicates several pages to nautical metaphors in Western approaches to poetic creation. Curtius cites everyone from the Roman poets Virgil and Horace to Saint Jerome, Dante and Spenser (Curtius 1991). When we are thinking about stories, it seems, we find ourselves drawn almost inexorably to thinking of the sea. And yet there is a difference between these Western texts and the Indian texts. In the former, the poet or the composer may be likened again and again to a navigator, but the journey is almost always ultimately considered as a passage from one shore to another. In the latter texts, on the other hand, it is no longer certain that there is any such thing as dry land: once we cast off on the ocean of stories, it seems that we may have to wave farewell to dry land for good.[4]

Armed with these propositions—that ethics is like navigation and stories are like the sea—it begins to become clear why it might be that, when it comes to making sense of the complex, shifting, sea-like nature of our existence, sometimes a story will get through where all of our philosophy, all of our analyses and proofs, seem to fail us. 'When experimentation doesn't get you there,' writes philosopher Michel Serres, 'let the story go there, if it can; if meditation fails, why not try narrative?' (Serres 1997, 165-6)

Or, to put it another way, if we are fated to live out our days adrift on the ocean, then hydrophobic dreams of dry land will do us no good. If we are to navigate with any degree of success, we cannot turn our backs upon the knowledge that is born from the changing winds and from the shifting of the tides. So let us cast off, then, upon these uncertain seas of stories; and let us see where we end up.

3

CASTING OFF

I t is winter. Outside, sleet is spattering against the window. I am sitting in the armchair and I am tired. Tired and ill-tempered.

You look at me. 'Tell me a story,' you say.

I do not want to tell you a story. 'I am too tired,' I say.

'Tell me a story,' you repeat.

I try to tell you that a story requires effort, that I have had a hard day... But as I am explaining all this, I realise that you are not going to give up, and that it would be easier, all things considered, to get on with it and tell a story. 'What story do you want to hear?' I sigh.

You smile. 'Tell me about Kikori and Fly,' you suggest. And so I do.[1]

Kikori and Fly

Kikori and Fly live in a cave. It is dark and unpleasant; and one day Kikori, tired of these conditions, has a thought: 'I will invent a house!' he says.

'What's a house?' asks Fly.

'I don't know,' Kikori confesses, 'I've not invented it yet.'

At this point, you smile and my exhaustion lifts a little.

Kikori goes into the forest. He cuts down some saplings, strips the trunks and makes poles. He takes some creepers and weaves them into strong ropes. Then he sets about building his house, binding the poles together with the ropes he has made.

Fly watches. 'All that effort, Kikori!' he says. 'I'll show you how to make a house.' And he buzzes out of the cave and starts to build a house of his own, moulding mud until he has a cosy shelter. It takes all of an hour before it is completed, but it is several days before Kikori has finished his labours. Fly sits in his mud house and taunts Kikori. 'You could copy me,' he says, 'if your pride did not prevent you.'

When at last Kikori's house is finished, the two friends settle down to life outside the cave.

Here I think of Plato, because a philosopher must always think of Plato at the mention of a cave. It is the law. A thought crosses my mind: are Kikori and Fly now two philosophers, recently emerged into the sunlight? But then I remind myself that caves existed before Plato, and they will continue to exist after Plato is forgotten. Sometimes a cave is just a cave. Besides, you are looking at me strangely, wondering why I have paused. I continue with the story.

Then the rains begin. A single drop, then two, then three, then a regular pattering. 'Come and stay with me,' calls Kikori to Fly, 'let us sit out the rainy season together.' But Fly refuses.

The rain becomes heavier, and Fly feels something fall on

the top of his head. He looks up: a drip. 'Kikori!' he calls from his door. 'Do you have a drip in your house?'

'Not yet, Fly,' Kikori replies.

There is another drip, then another. A damp patch is spreading through Fly's roof. There is a rumble of thunder.

'Friend Fly, come and spend the rains with me!' Kikori shouts from his doorway.

'No chance,' Fly replies. But then something terrible and large and black descends upon him. For a moment he wonders whether he has died. He wriggles and kicks. He is suffocating. What witchcraft is this? Then his head pokes back up into the daylight, and he looks around. He has no house. There is only a pool of mud.

Kikori begins to laugh. Fly sits brooding on his pile of dirt. And there he remains until this day. Kikori has long since lost patience with him. Now, when Fly comes buzzing into the house of Kikori's descendants, he is swatted away with an irritable hand.

The story is over. I sit back in my chair and fall silent. 'Thank you,' you say. 'I like that one.'

I say nothing. It is tiring work telling a story, and often it is hard to know what to say or do next. So we sit in silence. You glance out of the window. I think of Kikori constructing his idyll out there in the forest somewhere.

'Tell me another,' you say.

Prince Red Peter

All right. A story. Once again. Is there ever any end to this game of telling stories? Probably not. As Tristram Shandy knew, there is neither an end nor a beginning.[2]

'Which story do you want me to tell now?' I ask.

'Your choice,' you say.

I wait for a story to come to me and pick up my mug of tea. The tea is cold. I take a sip anyway. 'All right,' I say. 'How about Prince Red Peter?'[3]

You smile in agreement and close your eyes.

When Prince Red Peter was still a young man, his father offered him his inheritance. The prince, being prudent, buried the gold. Then he wished his father well and saddled his horse.

'Where are you going?' asked his father.

'Here I will become old, as you are old,' the prince replied. 'I am going to find a place free of death.'

So the prince travelled west for seven years. At last, he came to a vast forest. Several days' ride later, he heard a hammering and looked up to see a woodpecker clinging to the trunk of an old tree. 'Who are you?' Prince Red Peter asked.

'I am the King of the Wood,' the woodpecker replied. 'Who are you?'

'My name is Prince Red Peter. I am looking for a place beyond death.'

The woodpecker cocked his head. 'Then stay,' he said, 'for nobody in my kingdom will die until the last twig is pecked away.'

Prince Red Peter shook his head. 'Thank you,' he said, 'but that day will surely come.' Tipping his hat, he rode onwards.

Seven years later he came to a great plain encircled by seven mountains. At the foot of the mountains was a copper palace. Prince Red Peter knocked on the door. A beautiful young woman answered. 'Welcome,' she said. 'Please do come in.'

The prince spent the night in the copper palace. The girl

(who was, of course, a princess) fed him, gave him wine and chastely kissed him good night. The following day she asked him to stay. 'If you remain here and become my husband,' she said, 'you will not die until the mountains are worn away by the wind and the rain.'

But Prince Red Peter shook his head. 'That day too will come,' he said.

Seven years later he arrived at the edge of the world. His beard was already flecked with grey. Two mountains stood before him, the mountain on the left made of silver and the mountain on the right of gold. Between the two was a cave from out of which came a terrible howling. The prince dismounted from his horse, approached the cave and called out: 'Who's there?'

'Prince Red Peter! I am the West Wind! Welcome to the edge of the world. Why have you come this far?'

'I am looking for a place free of death,' the prince said.

And the West Wind replied, 'Then stay. Here you will neither age nor die. You may hunt on the golden mountain and you may hunt on the silver mountain and you will never grow old. But do not go into the Valley of Regret that lies in between.'

So Prince Red Peter made his home on the edge of the world. He drank from the fresh streams. His hair and beard turned jet-black again; his skin became like that of a lad still in his teenage years. One million years turned in their cycle. He hunted on the golden mountain. He hunted on the silver mountain. He did not go into the Valley of Regret.

I glance up. You are looking out of the window. The sleet continues to splatter against the panes, blurring the light from the street-lamps. I continue with the story.

~

One morning, he saw a stag on the mountainside, the most beautiful creature he had ever seen. He turned his horse and raised his bow. The stag dived into the trees and the prince gave chase.

The day was hot and the stag ran fast. The prince was so filled with the exhilaration of the hunt that he did not notice when the stag began to plunge down the steep slopes to the valley below. The prince followed for more than an hour before he heard the sound of trickling water. He hesitated. The stag crashed through the undergrowth and was gone.

Prince Red Peter looked down at the stream running by his feet. He could descend no more, for there was nowhere lower in the whole world. For the first time in one million years, he thought with a pang of longing of the princess in the copper palace. He remembered the woodpecker and wished that he could return to that wood. He recollected his city and thought that he would be truly happy if he could set eyes upon it again.

Taking leave of the wind, he made his way back east. After seven years, he came to an enormous plain in the middle of which was a weathered green hut. An old woman was seated outside. 'Old woman,' he said, 'what are you doing here?' 'Prince Red Peter?' the woman smiled. 'It is me, the princess. How quickly the years pass. Please, kiss me.'

Prince Red Peter leaned to kiss the old woman. His lips touched her cheek, she let out the lightest of sighs, and she fell dead at his feet.

He buried the princess and continued east for seven more years until he passed through a great wilderness almost devoid of life. There he heard a feeble tapping, like an old man walking with a cane, and he saw a small and shabby bird, almost featherless, wearily tapping at a stick with its beak. The bird looked up. 'Prince Red Peter! How soon the time goes...'

The King of the Wood pecked once more at the stick, and then he too fell down dead.

Prince Red Peter dug a second grave and continued on his journey.

After seven more years he came to a city he did not recognise, made of glass and steel. The air was foul to breathe. It was dusk, and the prince had nowhere else to go, so he took refuge in a park. As he was settling down to sleep on a bench, an old tramp came up to him. 'That's my bench.'

'Sorry,' mumbled the prince, and he stood up.

The tramp sat down and glowered. 'Who are you, foreigner?'

'My name is Prince Red Peter,' replied the prince.

'You're taking the piss, mate,' the tramp said. 'My mother used to tell me that story when I was a kid. She said the palace was here, in this very park. Buggered if I believe it. Now piss off. I want a kip.'

Leaving the tramp, Prince Red Peter wandered through the park. As he walked he began to recognise the remnants of his home—a wall here, a stone there—until at last he found himself standing by the place where, so long before, he had buried his inheritance. The moon was rising. He took a flat stone from the flowerbed and started to dig. Before long, he struck something solid. He cleared the earth and saw an old chest. It was unlocked. He lifted the lid slowly.

Inside were two dark shapes. The leftmost rose up before him, an old woman dressed in black. 'Peter,' she said, 'my name is Old Age. Come.' She took his hand.

Prince Red Peter's hair turned from black to grey to white. His skin shrivelled and his spine twisted. The old woman blurred into the night and Prince Red Peter's sight faded.

Then the second shape arose, a vague shadow now. 'Peter,' she said, 'my name is Death. Welcome. I've been waiting a long time.' And when she took his hand, Prince Red Peter's body crumbled away until it was nothing but dust in the moonlight.

~

I finish the story. Looking out of the window at the city in winter, I notice the moon over the rooftops. You don't say a word.

I look down at my watch. 'Is that the time?' I ask.

You shrug. 'Yes,' you say. 'We should probably get some sleep...'

What are Stories Good For?

The tough-minded philosopher, etymologically the lover of wisdom, might be tempted to respond to stories such as these by saying: this is all very well, but this is hardly the kind of thing that befits a serious philosopher. Stories are for those who are not up to the difficult job of philosophy. They are for children in whom reason has yet to harden. Or they are for those in whom reason has curdled—lunatics, the insane and certain foolish lovers. Or else they are for those in whom, the philosophers judge, reason has no hope of hardening—savages and simpletons, women, foreigners. Or they are for those in whom reason has long softened—the old and senile, those dulled by the practice of religion, or by hard labour. *It is only a story*, the philosophers say, and stories are not for the likes of philosophers. In the same way that Bernard of Clairvaux admitted that carvings in churches might have some use in teaching the foolish and illiterate masses, but they had no place in the cloister,[4] so the philosophers might permit some kind of subsidiary role for stories for those incapable of following the abstruse lines of real philosophical argument, but only as a concession to the feebleness of other minds.

Yet when we put to one side philosophical prejudices against such naïve means of reflection, and ask what actually goes on in the exchanging of tales such as these, we find that things become considerably more interesting. What are stories good for? Well, for a start, they can be remarkably productive of fresh knowledge. There is much to be discovered in a good story: more, sometimes, than can be found in endless piles of theory, or in whole shelves of abstruse philosophical analysis. For example, we know from the story of Kikori and Fly something of what it is like to invent, and what an extraordinary thing it is to bring something into being that did not exist before. We know that most worthwhile endeavours take considerable effort, and that shirking such effort may not be worth it in the long run. We know something about how to construct a shelter in the rainforests of Papua New Guinea, knowledge that may—who can say?—be of immeasurable value to us one day, that may even save our life or the lives of those we love. We know what it is like to be in a mudslide, and can perhaps from here infer something of what it is like to be in a landslide or an avalanche. The list could go on. None of this knowledge is certain, of course; but it is all, at least, *testable* against what we already know of the world, the kind of knowledge that, as the anthropologist Claude Lévi-Strauss once wrote, is 'good to think with.'

Similarly, from the story of Prince Red Peter, we know a little more about what it is like to live always in the shadow of death. We know something of princesses and their ways. We may have gained a little more knowledge about woodpeckers. We know that eternity cannot satisfy and that those things for which we long are precisely the things that are mortal and subject to change. We know that some tramps are extremely territorial when it comes to their park benches and that they sometimes use language that appears vulgar when used in a work of philosophy. None of this knowledge is absolute or certain. It is always subject to qualification and amendment. Some tramps might be generous in sharing their benches. Some tramps might even be philosophers, after the model of Diogenes. Not all princesses are alike. And so on. But this concern with absolute knowledge is the very thing that, in renouncing dreams of dry land, we must place to one side. Serres writes, 'We always assume that we don't know, or else that we know everything, yea or nay. Whereas commonly we know a bit, a meagre amount, enough, quite a bit' (Serres 1995, 5). Here, between absolute ignorance and absolute knowledge, in the place in-between where we all live and where we all die, stories speak to us.

However, we should not fall into thinking that, when it comes to the kind of knowledge we can glean from stories, absolutely anything goes. Some methods of building a shelter in the forests of Papua New Guinea, we now know, work well; others do not. There are some ways in which it is appropriate to address princesses, and other ways that are generally better avoided. To respond to a story wisely, we must see how the new knowledge gained takes its part within the greater framework of what knowledge—perhaps even what wisdom—we already possess, we must stitch and unstitch, weaving new understandings into the fabric of the knowledge of our lives.

But because this process of weaving and unweaving is an active, unstable process, stories cannot be just reduced down to lists of things that are knowable. Stories are more than simply mnemonics or coded propositions about the world.[5] Moralists everywhere love to relate stories and then to append morals to the end, as if the story was merely a colourful illustration of the moral. But as Kierkegaard—a philosopher who knew a thing or two about stories, and who knew enough to mistrust the moralists—once said, it is a supremely difficult thing to tell a story and to give the story its due.[6]

A story is not just the summing up of a moral, but it is also a kind of *casting-off*. We find ourselves caught up in its eddies and currents; we journey on whether with reluctance, with fear, or in the spirit of high adventure; and along the way, if we remain attentive, something emerges out of the telling that could not have been anticipated, something—all you stern and fearful moralists beware!—absolutely unforeseeable.

Nevertheless, it might be protested that at least on the surface of it, the two tales related here—the tale of Kikori and Fly, and the tale of Prince Red Peter—do not seem to have much to do with *philosophy*. Looking more closely, it will appear that they deal with themes that—when abstracted and translated into philosophical jargon—are familiar from a reading of the philosophers. We could say, for example, that the story of Kikori and Fly is concerned with the separation of cultural and natural worlds, with questions of human labour, with themes of exposure, security and hospitality. We could claim that the tale of Prince Red Peter deals with our nature as temporal beings, with our human relationship with death, with the paradoxes occasioned by the human desire for immortality. But we would have to also confess that these stories also deal with subjects upon which the philosophers rarely dwell: woodpeckers, for example, do not feature strongly in the Western (or, as far as I know, any other) philosophical canon. If Plato (unlikely) or Aristotle (not quite as unlikely, but still improbable) ever wrote a treatise on woodpeckers, it has been lost to history.[7]

But when confronted with stories such as these, the temptation for the philosopher is always to reduce the story down to its 'philosophical' bare bones, stripping it of everything that seems superficially 'unphilosophical.' Along the way, the woodpeckers are evicted, and having pared the story back to what is assumed to be its philosophical core, the resulting philosophy finds itself merely repeating the dogmas that we have learned to repeat from our reading of the philosophical texts. Such an approach fails to yield anything new. In our obsession with the abstract nouns of the philosophical lexicon, in our mania for generality that reduces 'woodpecker' down to the apparently more essential 'bird', 'bird' down to the apparently more essential 'non-human other', we end up losing all particularity, and learn nothing much new either about woodpeckers or about our philosophical categories. When this happens, everywhere we look, we find ourselves seeing the same thing. How, then, could our philosophy be wrong? But, on the other hand, how much have we missed—woodpeckers, flies squatting on piles of mud, tramps stretching out on park benches, princes, rainforests, mountains, cities, kingdoms—merely for the sake of being able to assert that our philosophy is right?

If we want to keep a place in the world—and in our thinking about morality—for woodpeckers and rainforests (and flies and tramps and cities and kingdoms and mountains), then perhaps we need to cast off from the philosophical obsession with absolute certainty, and to set out on the sea of stories. Through stories, through reflections upon stories, through stories about reflection, through stories about stories: by these means it may be possible to think about ethics in new ways.

It may be objected that this is not philosophy at all, that this is a rejection of philosophy altogether. It may be said that such an approach, in not giving us any dry ground to stand upon, leads to circularity. But when we have renounced our hopes of philosophical dry land, then there is nowhere to stand that is outside of circles such as these, and there never was. We can only hope that the circles are not vicious, or at the very least, that they are circles in which we can find ways of quelling our viciousness.[8] And if charged to say why this still might merit the name 'philosophy', the best answer I can give is that, whatever else, it is an approach that maintains some kind of belief that wisdom—even a little wisdom, whatever wisdom may turn out to be—might be a thing worth having, a thing worthy of our love and of our cherishing.

~

You look at me. 'Tell me a story,' you say.

   I do not want to tell you a story. 'I am too tired,' I say.

   'Tell me a story,' you repeat.

   And so I begin.

4

STORYTELLING AND EXPERIENCE

There may be few things more familiar to us than the telling of stories, and no way of thinking more natural to us than story-thinking. And yet it is not at all clear what kind of thinking it is that goes on in stories.[1] As is often the case, the sheer everyday mundaneness of telling stories is the very thing that makes it a strangely difficult process to get to grips with. One thing, however, seems to me to be clear: that if we do want to understand storytelling better, we need to do far more than look at stories in isolation—as cold corpses laid out on the slab as we sharpen the tools of our literary analysis. We also need to attend to the living, breathing complexity of the telling. A story is not just something that we can carve up in this way or that to extract meanings and propositions; it is also something that we experience *being told*.

Hatching the Egg of Experience

The German philosopher and literary critic Walter Benjamin was profoundly fascinated by the nature of storytelling, and by the relationship between storytelling and experience. In his

1936 essay 'The Storyteller', Benjamin explores how the decline in storytelling in the late nineteenth and early twentieth centuries can be correlated with the way in which experience has 'fallen in value'. He conjures up the image of the broken armies of survivors who came back from the front of the First World War 'grown silent—not richer but poorer in communicable experience' (Benjamin 2006, 144): it was not stories with which the survivors returned, but instead a terrible and deep silence.

When Benjamin talks about experience, he is not talking about what philosophers often mean by the term. He is not talking about the first-person 'view from within', the seemingly irreducible coffee-ness that we experience when we drink coffee, the painfulness of pain, the redness of red, the 'me-ness' of being me. It is less the kind of experience that we talk about when we say 'my toothache last week was not a pleasant experience,' and more the kind of experience that we are talking about when we say 'don't worry—the pilot is very experienced!'[2] The usual philosopher's idea of experience as something inward tends to separate us out from the world, to set us apart. Benjamin's approach to experience, on the other hand, serves to bind us to the world, bringing to light the many relationships we have with it. Experience, seen in this light, is something richly interwoven, something formed through, 'a learning process over time, combining negations through unpleasant episodes as well as affirmations through positive ones'. And this weaving of experience is capable of producing 'something akin to a wisdom that can be passed down via tradition through the generations' (Jay 1998, 195).

This is a far richer understanding of experience than that traditionally offered by the philosophers. The old philosophical story that the world is made up of subjects with inner experience who face objects in the external world seems, when set against the story that Benjamin tells about experience, decidedly impoverished. And while it is true that sometimes we do experience ourselves as subjects facing an objective world, it is also true that—as Howard Caygill writes while discussing Benjamin's work—this philosophical notion of experience is only 'one of many possible surfaces of experience' (Caygill 1997, 24). Much of our experience simply does not conform to the model of objects and subjects: the experience of 'flow' as one skis down a hill; the experience of playing in an orchestra; the experience of daydreaming while the cat purrs on one's lap; the experience of driving a car down a familiar country lane and finding ourselves all of a sudden back at home, without being able to recollect anything of the journey; experiences of fever and of sickness; or, perhaps, the experience of dozing on the grass on a summer's afternoon. Benjamin's contemporary, Franz Rosenzweig, goes as far to claim that much of our experiencing has very little to do with objects at all—or, for that matter, with subjects. Rosenzweig writes as follows:

> Experience knows nothing of objects; it remembers, it experiences, it hopes and fears [...] it is nothing but a prejudice of the last three centuries that in all knowledge the "I" must necessarily accompany it; so that I would not be able to see any tree without the "I" seeing it. In truth my I is only present when it—is present; when, for instance, I must stress that I see the tree because someone else does not see it; then certainly the tree in my knowledge is bound up with me; but in all other cases I only know of the tree and of nothing else; and the standard philosophical claim that the I is omnipresent in all knowledge distorts the content of this knowledge (Rosenzweig 1998, 80).

What this all implies is that experience may be a more complex affair than many philosophers like to pretend. When I sit looking at the light on the poplar tree out of the window, there is certainly some kind of *experiencing* going on; but to describe this in terms of a relationship between an absolutely distinct subject and an absolutely distinct object, as the philosophers would have it, seems to capture little of the nature of this experience. For much of the time, while I know that there is some kind of experiencing going on (I must be experiencing the car that hurtles down the street, because I step aside and take evasive action), it is not clear that I am consciously aware of everything that I am experiencing (I don't even notice that I am stepping aside to avoid the car) or aware of myself as the 'owner' of these experiences. It is only when somebody asks 'What are you doing?' that I find myself saying, 'I am avoiding the car,' or 'I am looking at the tree.' In this moment my 'I' is present; but until that moment, while there is indeed experience, it is hard to say where the demarcation line is between the experiencing subject and the experienced object. At times such as these, it can seem as if, although there is experience, there isn't really anybody doing the experiencing.

Following Benjamin and Rosenzweig as they move away from this more traditional philosophical story about the nature of experience allows us to see that experience itself is something richer and more interwoven than we might formerly have allowed. It is not so much a single relationship as—to steal Rushdie's resonant phrase—a *liquid tapestry* in constant motion.

This particular story about experience seems to me to be a generous one because in recognising that we are not tightly-bound subjects facing off against an objective world, it allows for the possibility of a kind of freedom within experience. Experience is perhaps *un*woven as much as it is woven, shot through with 'unexpected transitions,' transitions that are made possible precisely because of the 'gaps, warps or breaks in the continuity of experience' (Caygill 1997, 26-7).

While this may seem a little esoteric, it is also decidedly

everyday. When one puts to one side the fictions of ideal philosophical subjects, and simply pays attention to these many surfaces of experience, it begins to become apparent that this apparently seamless and well-ordered experience is gappy, badly-patched, and cobbled-together. We move through the world acting and thinking and perceiving, but our thinking and acting and perceiving are not things that are co-ordinated tightly together. We are multiple channels of streaming information, knitted together in a single body. And not only does our experience often seem to be rather different from the notion of experience developed by the philosophers, sometimes it also doesn't even seem to be 'ours', except in a rather minimal sense: for example, the non-experience of the road home, when the mind is elsewhere. Sometimes philosophers like to talk about the self-evidence of experience. When one starts to look at the many everyday stories that we tell ourselves and each other about what experience is really like, and when one pays attention to the breathtakingly varied texture and form of these stories, this supposedly self-evident experience seems to be rather less evident, and rather less selfy, than the philosophers might like.

Perhaps, then, when it comes to getting some kind of purchase on what it means to have experience at all, stories may get through where our attempts at analysis fail. But the telling of tales is neither a way of imposing some ideal order upon this shifting patchwork of experience nor is it an activity that is separate from this patchwork. Instead, it is itself an interwoven experience that, in its unfolding, weaves, unweaves and reweaves the liquid tapestry of experience.[3]

It is no accident that the metaphor of weaving also appears in Benjamin's essay, where he relates the continual weaving of experience to the idea of wisdom. The impoverishment of experience in the wake of the First World War, Benjamin writes, is also a loss of the 'counsel woven into the fabric of real life' (Benjamin 2006, 146)—a form of counsel that Benjamin identifies with wisdom. This counsel is not some set of ethical maxims that tell us how or how not to act—here there are no clear injunctions about selling one's hair, masturbation or telling lies—but is instead 'a proposal concerning the continuation of a story that is in the process of unfolding' (Benjamin 2006, 145-6). Benjamin is not talking about wisdom as anything absolute or unworldly but is instead referring to something rather more down-to-earth. We know more about wisdom than we think. We know, for example, when one of our friends jumps into the polar bear's enclosure at the zoo for a photo-opportunity and a hug, that this act is unwise. And, conversely, we recognise the wisdom of another friend who, after long conversation, speaks a single sentence that allows us to see our own lives in a new and fruitful light.

These references to weaving in Benjamin's essay are much more than idle metaphors, for Benjamin goes on to point out that storytelling is 'itself an artisanal form of communication' (Benjamin 2006, 149): a kind of communication that, like all artisanal work, requires time for its flourishing.[4] The weaving of stories is closer to the work of the loom and of the hand than we often are willing to credit. When we find ourselves stuck on a station platform awaiting a train that never comes, when the good people of Florence in Boccaccio's *Decameron* take refuge from the plague in the country, when a prisoner is trapped within their cell with more time on their hands than they know what to do with, or when somebody hands us a bowl of peas to shell—it is at these times that we find ourselves turning to the telling of stories. For, as Benjamin memorably writes, 'boredom is the dream bird that hatches the egg of experience. A rustling in the leaves drives him away' (Benjamin 2006, 149). And when the dream bird—woodpecker or sparrow, vulture or phoenix—has flown the nest, when there is no egg to hatch, what hope do we have of wisdom?

Speech Thinking

Benjamin arranges the threads of his argument in such a way as to persuade us that there may be connections between story-telling, the weaving of experience and wisdom. Not only this, he also suggests that wisdom is the kind of thing that cannot be won too quickly: here is a dish that needs to be cooked over a slow fire. And while Benjamin hints about the specifically ethical implications of this kind of weaving of experience and of wisdom, the connections between storytelling and ethics are made much more explicit in the work of Rosenzweig.

We have already seen that philosophy—at least in the West —has frequently concerned itself with finding solid ground, with seeking immutable and unchanging truths. For Rosen-zweig, there is something disturbing in the tendency that philosophy has toward looking beyond the flux and change of the world, renouncing the world in which we are immersed in favour of dreams of things that are eternal and unchanging. In aspiring to think timelessly—in what Rosenzweig terms the 'cognition of the All'—philosophy has frequently missed the very things that (as we know from Aristotle) are most important when it comes to ethics: our own particularity and the particu-larity of others, the fine grain of experience, the small-print of our lives. 'Only the singular can die and everything mortal is solitary,' Rosenzweig writes, '[p]hilosophy has to rid the world of what is singular' (Rosenzweig 1985, 4). That is to say that, the philosopher is a figure not unlike the knight in Bergman's *Seventh Seal* who challenges Death to a game of chess, and who believes that he can win. On the chessboard, he notes, there are knights, but there is no piece for Death... so how could he possibly lose? Yet he eventually finds that there is no winning against this particular opponent and that at the game's ending he too must join the merry dance over the hill.

For Rosenzweig, the error that is repeated throughout the

Western philosophical tradition is this: it has set its eyes on finding a kind of timelessness that might rob the abstraction Death of its sting, but this very aspiration—itself rooted in a fear of death—tends to obscure the very real deaths that we all must suffer.[5] 'Death,' as Allen Ginsberg wrote in his travel diaries from India, 'is not a single thing' (Ginsberg 1996, 199). In this way, Rosenzweig insists, philosophy has little to say about our own individual deaths, and in turning away from one of the things that we most fear, it 'plugs up its ears before the cry of terrorised humanity' (Rosenzweig 1985, 5).

There are two distinct problems here. The first is epistemological, which is to say, it is a problem concerning our knowledge of things. The mania for abstractions and universals is one that risks becoming inattentive to the phenomena of this world, to the fragile, labile, changeable world in which we live. Philosophy evicts the woodpeckers and gains little in return. The second problem is ethical. The concern that we have (perhaps in ethics more than anywhere else) with universal knowledge can lead us to ignore what is most present and most urgent. It is relatively easy to think about ethics, to philosophise about ethics, to write books and treatises, to attend learned symposia or to mount the steps that lead to the pulpit and there to speak movingly and passionately to the gathered crowds about how we might act for the better. But it is a riskier thing to actually respond to the naked need of another human being.

As a means of breaking with this habit of fleeing particular circumstances for dreams of universality, Rosenzweig proposes a new kind of philosophy 'based on experience' (Mendes-Flohr, 2006). Yet this new kind of philosophy turns out to also be a very old kind of philosophy: the method that Rosenzweig proposes is that of storytelling.[6] Stories, Rosenzweig maintains, allow us to think about time precisely because there are no short-cuts when it comes to telling a story. 'To cut a long story short...' we say; and yet we also know that stories take time, that if we are about to tell or hear a story, we might as well cancel our appointments and make ourselves comfortable. It will take as long as it takes. Stories are bound to time and nourished by time, and as stories unfold, they have the effect of restoring to us our sense of how our existence is itself both bound to and nourished by time. For Rosenzweig, this return to a sense of ourselves as subject to time—as living, breathing creatures who were born, who live, and who will die—is an essential stage in opening the way to the possibility of ethics[7] Rosenzweig contrasts the kind of thinking favoured by the philosophers— which he calls 'thinking thinking' or 'logical thinking'—with the kind of thinking that goes on in the telling of stories— which he calls 'speaking thinking' or 'grammatical thinking'— in the following way:

> The thinker plainly knows his thoughts in advance; that he 'expresses' them is only a concession to the defectiveness, as he calls it, of our means of communication; this does not consist in the fact that we need speech, but rather in the fact that we need time. To need time means: not to be able to presuppose anything, to have to wait for everything, to be dependent on the other for what is ours. All this is entirely unthinkable to the thinking thinker, while it alone suits the speech-thinker—for of course the new, speaking-thinking is also thinking, just as the old, the thinking thinking did not come about without inner speaking; the difference between the old and new, logical and grammatical thinking, does not lie in sound and silence, but in the need of an other and, what is the same thing, in the taking of time seriously. Here, 'thinking' is taken to mean thinking for no one and speaking to no one (for which, you can substitute 'everyone,' the so-called 'general public,' if you think it sounds better). But speaking means to speak to someone and to think for someone; and this Someone is always a very definite

Someone, and doesn't merely have ears like the general public, but also a mouth. (Rosenzweig 1998, 86-7)

Philosophy, in other words, is not only an attempt to think timelessly, but also to think outside of community and outside of history. In the middle of the seventeenth century, Descartes retires to his study and attempts to put all popular opinions, all knowledge gained from hearsay and all counsel from others, to one side, so that he might start from scratch in constructing an edifice of pure and unsullied thought. Whatever the merits of such a withdrawal, when it comes to thinking about ethics, this is hardly a model for the budding philosopher to follow. That is to say, ethics is an issue precisely *because* we live in community with others, precisely *because* we are historical beings subject to time's passing.[8] So to think about ethics, Rosenzweig might maintain, it is necessary to break down the study door, to return to the circle of people huddled around the fire, weaving cloths or shelling peas, and there—in community with others —to begin with a story. Stories live in the telling and in the retelling. And here, around the fire, we may find flooding back into our ethical reflection all of those things that the philosophers have so long excluded: our passions and loves, our uncertainties, our contradictions and our confusions, the profuse multiplicity of our existence.

We live and breathe through stories, and it has been justly said that our species could be characterised as *Homo narrans* (Niles 1999). But that is not to say that our lives *are* stories or that they are story-like in structure. The stories that we weave are multiple, fragmentary, interlocking, in constant motion. We are not stories, but we are ourselves seas of stories, or else we are eddies in the larger sea of stories of which we are a part.[9] But the stories that we habitually weave are neither single nor do they have the tidy structure of beginning, middle and end that Aristotle claimed was the mark of a good story. Instead, they are a morass of innumerable, half-cooked drafts that contradict and overlap and flow around each other in ceaseless motion. To observe more closely the ebb and flow of our ordinary everyday experience, its undertows and riptides and doldrums, we need to pay attention to our natures as storytelling creatures, without allowing our stories to become single, or attempting to reduce experience down to a simple philosophical structure.

Such close attention towards experience—forgetting about timeless essences and paying attention instead to the messiness of the everyday flux, the riot of appearances in the world—could be called a kind of phenomenology, an approach to philosophy in which one puts to one side questions about timeless essences and asks 'what is it actually *like* to experience something-or-other?'[10] By carefully attending to experience as it unfolds, this approach to philosophy may be able to say things about the world and about ourselves that other approaches have overlooked. Yet it should also be said that a phenomenology that proceeds by spinning tales and yarns looks, from a philosophical point of view, to be a very curious kind of phenomenology indeed.

A Curious Kind of Phenomenology

Perhaps it is not the oldest philosophical question in the book, but it is one of the most recurrent, at least once puberty has kicked in: 'What is this thing called love?' In the form in which it is phrased, this is almost the paradigmatically philosophical form of questioning: 'What is x?'—where x can stand for any abstraction that you like. One could call such questions Socratic, for they seek the kind of certain ground for which Socrates was seeking. One could also call them *difficult* questions, for it is not at all clear how we could go about answering them. How on earth *does* one find an answer to the question

'What is this thing called love?' Should we scour the dictionaries and our reference books? Should we seek out experts in love to consult? Should we perform a little distillation in the laboratory, extracting test-tube after test-tube of potent pheromones? Should we put on a recording of Ella Fitzgerald to remind ourselves whether she provides us with an answer, or whether she just continually reiterates the question? Or should we gaze into the middle-distance and conjure up loveless abstractions about the nature of love, arguing and debating late into the night? And were we to debate in this fashion, when the sun eventually rose the following morning, would we find that we had come to a clear and unambiguous understanding of the essence of love, or would we instead have gained little else other than thumping headaches and new, unlovely animosities?

If philosophy traditionally specialises in difficult questions, storytelling tends to explore easier questions: not 'What is this thing called love?' but 'What is love *like*?' It is this shift in the kinds of question asked that makes storytelling a kind of phenomenology. The moment we seek to answer the question 'What is love like?', we find we have already cast off upon the sea of stories, animated and alive, craning forwards as we speak, gesticulating wildly, attentive to both the tale and to our audience.

Q: What is love like?

A: Well, let me tell you. I was twenty-two years old, and I was travelling through Rome on the way to Sorrento. I met her sitting by a fountain in the sunshine, and somehow we got talking. Her name was Florencia, and she was from Argentina. We spoke about Borges as we shared bread and cheese in the spring afternoon...

Or instead of weaving a story, we might conjure up images, fragments and drafts of possible stories: love is like a burning furnace, like a hot air balloon, like a murmur beneath the level of hearing, like a drunken astronaut dancing a solitary tango on the surface of the moon. And if we took this course, then by the following dawn—if we continued to ask these kinds of questions—although we would have nothing that resembled a definitive answer, at least we would not have headaches and animosity, and perhaps we might, without our even knowing it, have woven a little more counsel and—dare it be said?—also a little more love into the fabric of our lives.

Here, however, we need to be philosophically cautious.[11] The way that this second question is phrased, 'What is love like?' risks seducing us into thinking that there *is*, in fact, a single thing, love, towards which this new question will lead us. But the more we ask this kind of question, the more it becomes apparent that love is no more a single thing than is death. What emerges from our storytelling is not Love, but a multiplicity of loves. No story on earth has ever led to a clear and unassailable definition of any single bald abstraction such as 'love' or 'death' or 'justice.' Stories do not lead us back towards deep sources of ultimate meaning, but rather they lead us outward on new trajectories. You tell me, 'It was true love,' and you tell me almost nothing. So you take a deep breath and tell me the story of how you met on the Orient Express, of how you spent three glorious weeks together paddling down the Danube in your home-made canoe, how only once did you fall out (of harmony, that is, not out of the canoe), over the price of some tourist heirloom which neither of you really wanted anyway, and of how you parted—one to the north and the other to the south, without exchanging telephone numbers or addresses. And in the telling it seems as if something emerges that is quite new, something I could not have anticipated, something that is not reducible to knowledge, however many understandings it may nevertheless yield. In the process of relating this story of love along the length of a river into which it is absolutely certain that one can never step twice, if the story is told well and the conditions are right, a new idea of 'love' emerges like Venus rising from the foam, each time different from the last and from the next. And this is why Rosenzweig can say that stories, like conversations, always threaten or promise to deliver us to places we could not have anticipated in advance—even, or perhaps especially, when the story is 'known' to us.

So it is not a question of asking 'what is this thing called love?' nor is it even a question of asking 'what is love like?'—a question that risks seducing us into the belief that there is single essence of love that we can grasp hold of. Instead we need to cast ourselves adrift on the Danube, with or without a canoe, and surrendering ourselves to the flow of the river, to ask a third question: 'What actually emerges when we talk about that which we designate (perhaps too hastily) as love?' or else, 'How does love emerge in our telling tales about love?' The thing we are trying to understand is not an essence to be grasped by apt analogical thinking but is instead something emergent in the telling. Somehow, as we follow the course of the river (into which it is probable that one cannot step even once),[12] as we relate the argument over the tourist tat, the parting, the journey that unfolds, something inessential, purely phenomenal, but something that we are content nevertheless to call love, is born. When this happens, our sense of what it may be that we are talking about when we talk about love begins to shift, to change, and to take on a new form.

Such a phenomenology is no doubt hopelessly naïve. In shying away from the difficult questions, it will be accused of ducking the major issues at stake, of losing nerve and dropping out of the two and a half thousand year old quest for philosophical certainty. It will be accused of being inconsistent, for it may rise not to a single result, but to many results, a proliferation of results that are far too diverse and unruly to be fashioned together into a system. Against these complaints, perhaps it is possible only to throw up our hands and to say, yes, this approach is naïve, to confess that yes, it risks inconsistency, to admit that, no, it will not provide us with certainty. And yet for all this, when a problem still seems without resolution after two and a half thousand years, it is not unreasonable to change tack and to ask some different kinds of questions.

5

A NAÏVE PHENOMENOLOGY OF ETHICS

A
t this point, I want to return to the perplexing experience in the marketplace at Darjeeling with which I began. I have dwelt at some length upon the uncertainty in ethics and the fluidity of experience, but I have not forgotten the other curiously unarguable aspect of this experience in the marketplace: the recurrent and unshakable sense that *we should have done something*. This is something that I find it impossible to remove from my memory of that morning in the bazaar. The moment that the man looked directly at me, the moment in which he turned his eyes towards me, had to it all the force of an imperative. But it was an imperative that I ignored, asking myself *what could I have done*?

The Experiential Imperative

If I have returned to this recollection again and again in the years that have followed, it has not been in the spirit of morbid and relentless self-recrimination, but rather in the spirit of investigation: for this experience seemed to me then—and still seems now—to be one that clearly dramatised something that far too much ethical philosophy overlooks. For if this was an imperative, as it indeed seemed to be, it was not the kind of imperative of which the philosophers are fond. It was certainly not the kind of imperative that is handed down by the moralists and lawmakers, nor was it the kind of imperative capable of being established, as Kant dreamed, by reason. The kinds of imperatives that are secured either by philosophical reason or by reference to authority may, of course, have some value either in thinking through ethics or in helping us to navigate through the world. But the kind of imperative I encountered that afternoon in the bazaar in Darjeeling was not really something that can be described in terms of reason or in terms of authority. It was an imperative woven into the heart of the experience itself, an *experiential* imperative that was striking in its immediacy.[1] If reason had a role to play in this particular set of events, it was not a particularly dignified or ennobling one. Confronted by the immediacy of this imperative, the voice of reason spoke up and said that there was so much suffering in the world anyway, that there was almost certainly nothing that could be done, and then—the immediacy of the imperative dulled a little by this kind of reasoning—in a moment we had gone on our way.

The fact that imperatives come to us not just from the lawgivers and the exercise of reason, but are instead woven directly into the fabric of experience itself, is one of the reasons that ethics badly needs a form of phenomenology, an attentiveness to the nature of ethical experience. While philosophers have complex ways of talking about ethics, they have paid very little attention to ethical *experience* itself—to the ways in which the eyes slide to one side when we want to sidestep our responsibilities, to the physical sensation in the chest when we encounter another's suffering, to the way that the hand instinctively reaches out to steady the person who stumbles in the street. If we wish to find accounts of these kinds of subtleties and complexities, then it is not the philosophers who speak most eloquently, but the novelists and the storytellers, the poets both known and unknown who are, as Shelley points out, the unacknowledged legislators of the world. And when the philosophers do manage to speak resonantly and most persuasively about matters of ethics, they do so in the form of stories and poems. Stories are phenomenologies.

In speaking of phenomenology at all, I am conscious that I cannot help but raise the shade of the philosopher Edmund Husserl. At the beginning of the twentieth century, Husserl—a philosopher of painstaking care and rigour—started the phenomenological movement that was to give birth to some immensely rich philosophical storytelling. Husserl's method was one of paying careful attention to questions of the form 'What is *x* like?' in the hope that, by means of describing with the utmost care the necessary structures of the consciousness, it might be possible at last to establish the kinds of certainties that had eluded the philosophers for so long. 'We entirely lack a rational science of man and of the human community,' Husserl complained in 1923, 'a science that would establish a rationality in social and political activity and a rational, political technique' (Husserl 1982, 328). Of all the philosophers of the twentieth century, none dreamed the dream of solid ground with more intensity than Husserl; and the complex phenomenological method that he dedicated his life to explaining was aimed at providing precisely the kind of rational science that would have solved, once and for all, the perplexities of Socrates and Euthyphro. And yet Husserl's hope was never realised. Like the rest of the prophets, the phenomenologists—amongst whom are counted many of the most creative and imaginative philosopher-storytellers of the twentieth-century, figures such as Heidegger, Merleau-Ponty, Sartre and Levinas—have seemed all but incapable of agreement on even the simplest of matters.

It is no easy thing, it turns out, to lay bare the necessary structures of consciousness. Benjamin and Rosenzweig's accounts of experience suggest that experience itself is a complex and slippery thing, something that doesn't neatly correspond to tidy philosophical categories and that may not, curiously, be as accessible to introspection as we might first believe. Nor is it certain, even if we were eventually successful in providing the kind of descriptive science of consciousness for which Husserl once hoped, that this by itself would be sufficient to provide firm foundations for those slippery questions of ethics and politics that confront us.[2] And so perhaps it is no surprise that Husserl towards the end of his career turned from a concern with philosophy as a pure and rigorous science to a concern with philosophy as something more akin to storytelling, even going so far as to refer to his later works, not without irony, as 'my novels' (Edie 1997, 120). Three years before his death, in an essay titled 'Denial of Scientific Philosophy', Husserl wrote the following melancholy line: 'Philosophy as a science, as serious, rigorous, indeed apodictically rigorous science—*the dream is over*' (Husserl 1970, 389). The philosopher-scientist becomes a philosopher-novelist, and Husserl, at the end of his career, finds what Aristotle also discovered many centuries before him: that the quest for wisdom has inexorably led him, in his old age, towards the shifting sea of stories.[3]

It may be, then, that storytelling can indeed function as a naïve kind of phenomenology; and also that phenomenology, as I have already suggested, may be best seen as a kind of storytelling. In this light, we can see the phenomenologists not as theorists who managed to put knowledge on new foundations, but as weavers of potent stories and myths that genuinely manage, through the depth and subtlety of their storytelling, to capture something of the *what it is like* of experience. To read philosophers as storytellers in this way can be a bracing exercise, one that frees us from the obligation that philosophers often put upon their readers: the all-or-nothing demand to either subscribe to the entire system, or else to go through the long labour of mustering legions of counter-arguments, just so we might secure for ourselves the opportunity to say something new.

It is in this spirit that I want to approach the philosopher, Emmanuel Levinas, who must be one of the most powerful of all storytellers of ethics. Levinas is a philosopher who gives us a profoundly visceral sense of the 'what it is like?' of at least some of the ethical imperatives that we experience. When I think back to that encounter in the foothills of the Himalayas, no philosopher, East or West, captures the sense of what was going on in that strange meeting as well as does Levinas.

Responsibility and Freedom

Born to Jewish parents in Kaunas, Lithuania, a student of both Husserl and Heidegger, Levinas became a naturalised French citizen in 1930. After the outbreak of the Second World War, Levinas enrolled in the French officer corps, and in 1940 he was interred in the Fallingsbotel prison labour camp, where he spent the remainder of the war, and where he made the notes that eventually became his first major philosophical work, *Existence and Existents*—a moving meditation on selfhood, suffering and the possibility of goodness.[4] But it is perhaps his later book, *Totality and Infinity*, first published in 1961, that has had the greatest influence, chiefly for the immensely powerful account that it gives of the ethical drama that occurs in our encounters with other human beings.

Levinas claims that in this book he is inspired by the criticisms Rosenzweig advances against the philosophical tradition, but he goes on to say that he intends to go about exploring these criticisms using the Husserl's methods. This seems an initially somewhat unpromising enterprise—something akin to curing a headache by a further blow to the head—as Husserl's dreams of certainty, it could be argued, are precisely the kind of thing in philosophy with which Rosenzweig is so uneasy. And yet, despite such curious beginnings, as he navigates between Rosenzweig and Husserl, Levinas develops a strange and fascinating kind of phenomenology that, while giving up on the idea of philosophical certainty, manages to probe away at some of the deepest questions concerning our relationships with others, speaking about ethical experience with a directness that is perhaps still unparalleled.

Levinas's starting point is an insight that he takes from Husserl. When we encounter another human being, Husserl tells us, phenomenologically speaking, we do not encounter them only as objects upon which we might stub our toes or which we might be able to manipulate, but we also encounter them as *subjects* (Husserl 1997, 91). In this encounter, the other person's subjectivity is always and forever inaccessible to us. As Levinas writes, the other person 'escapes my grasp by an essential dimension, even if I have him at my disposal' (Levinas 1969, 39). Hence the insecurity of lovers. 'Tell me you love me,' the lover pleads. 'I love you,' says the beloved. But how can the lover be sure? 'Tell me you *really* love me,' the lover persists. 'I *really* love you,' says the beloved. The lover chews upon his or her nails anxiously, and no amount of reassurance will overcome his or her anxiety.[5]

For Levinas, this fact of ungraspability, the fact that I cannot render the other person completely knowable, means that when I encounter another person, the blithe sense I have that I am the master of myself and of the world that I inhabit is called into question. In encountering the other person I encounter, in a sense, a limitation of my power: think of the shop-keeper who wryly complains that their shop would be perfectly orderly and their life entirely unruffled, were it not for the inconvenience of having customers. When there are others involved, there is always something beyond our grasp, something unforeseeable.

But what is it actually *like* to encounter another human being, to experience this ungraspability and this limitation of our power? To explore this question, let me go back to my description of that morning in Darjeeling. When writing about the man in the bazaar, I wrote that it was his face I remembered. In saying this, I certainly am not saying that I have an accurate recollection of his physiognomy. I do not remember the tilt of his chin, the colour of his eyes, the size of his nose. Were I to meet him again, I am almost certain I would not recognise him. But still, it seems to me as if I remember his face, even if I cannot fully articulate what I mean when I make this claim.

This curious and seemingly paradoxical idea of the 'face' is at the heart of Levinas's phenomenology of ethics. When we encounter the face of another, Levinas writes, this face is not the eyes, the forehead, the nose and the chin. Indeed, Levinas says that to encounter the face of another is 'not even to notice the colour of his eyes' (Levinas 1985, 85). Experience shows that it is precisely *when* we notice the colour of somebody's eyes or the spot on their chin or their curious earlobes, that we find ourselves falling momentarily out of the living relationship we have with them, losing the sense of the other *person* as another person. Attention to the other person as an object with certain objective properties tends to attenuate the sense we have of a living, social relationship; and conversely, the awareness we have of these objective qualities fades into the background as the social relationship takes hold. 'When one observes the colour of the eyes,' Levinas continues, 'one is not in social relationship with the Other.' Not only this, but this ordinary, everyday social experience is not one that is ethically neutral. It is not that we encounter others and that then ethics is somehow 'added on' to this encounter; but it is instead that our relationship with others is, as Levinas writes, 'straightaway ethical.' When I encounter another person, I find myself responsible for them—I find myself unable to do anything other than respond to them *as* another person—whether I like it or not. This is what I am trying to describe by writing of the experiential imperative that I encountered in the bazaar in Darjeeling: there is a demand upon us in our encounters with others that is woven into the heart of experience and is an ineradicable part of that experience. It is there whether or not we choose to assume the responsibilities that are incumbent upon us. We all know that we can very well respond to another by turning away from them and telling ourselves it is not our problem (as I did on that afternoon), or by harming them, or by seeking to destroy them. But even the desire to destroy another, for example, or to harm them, or to imprison them, is a desire that arises out of the fact that here, standing before us, is a fellow human being who is, in some sense, beyond our power.[6]

So the idea of the face in Levinas is an attempt to capture the phenomenology—the what is it like?—of being faced by another human being, and of experiencing them *as* another human being. It is, in this sense, something quite ordinary and everyday, as is the responsibility that I encounter in the face of the other person. But Levinas goes on to point out that even if I do choose to assume these responsibilities, it is not as if I can *discharge* them. In fact, the converse is true: the more I assume my responsibilities towards another, the more these responsibilities increase. Imagine for a moment that I had, in fact, gone over to the man in the marketplace at Darjeeling, that I had reached out to him. What then? In this very response, I would have become more bound up in the responsibilities incumbent upon me: first a few steps across the space of the bazaar; next the recognition that he is sick, perhaps; then the demand upon me to respond to this new knowledge, so that I might call a taxi to take us to the hospital; then the question of the hospital bills... There is no reason that this cycle of increasing responsibility should not continue indefinitely. In assuming the responsibilities I have towards another human being, I am not absolved of further responsibilities, but instead my responsibilities deepen.

This experience also is far from uncommon. Let us imagine another example. One day you are going home, and you see Mavis, a bad-tempered pensioner who is also your neighbour, struggling along the street with her shopping. Before you can stop yourself, and against your better judgement, you find yourself offering to help her. The next day when you see her, you are displeased to realise that the demands upon you are greater, not fewer: the experiential imperatives are more urgent and more compelling precisely because the day before you assumed the responsibilities that were incumbent upon you. There is Mavis with her shopping, and you *really* can't not help her after having helped her the day before... So once again you carry her shopping, and before you know it, you find that you are helping her unpack it when you get it home for her. Over the next few days, things begin to spiral out of control; by the time the week is out, you find yourself in Mavis's living room drinking a cup of weak tea and eating stale biscuits as she tells you interminably dull stories from the distant past. And you wonder: how did I end up here? The answer is that you ended up there precisely on account of the peculiar structure of responsibility that Levinas describes so well. Our responsibilities have the habit of increasing even more rapidly than we can assume them. We are, Levinas claims, infinitely responsible for the other person.

Levinas, however, presses the argument even further. For if we are *infinitely* responsible for the other person, then we are also infinitely responsible for *all* others. As Levinas explains, 'The infinity of responsibility denotes not its actual immensity, but a responsibility increasing in the measure that it is assumed; duties become greater in the measure that they are accomplished' (Levinas 1969, 244). In helping Mavis with her shopping, even as my responsibilities to her increase, I am at the same time defaulting on my responsibilities to the friend I should be meeting in the park, for whom I will now be late. And in meeting the friend in the park, I am guiltily aware that I am not doing a hundred other things that I really should be doing for a hundred other people. Unfortunately, however, I have only one pair of hands. I simply cannot avoid defaulting on my responsibilities, and the moment of betrayal is, Levinas insists, inevitable—something we can postpone but not eliminate (Levinas 1969, 236). I am never in a situation that I can claim to have done absolutely everything that is to be done. I never reach a point at which I can sit on my laurels and say, 'I have done all that I can.' If all of this seems terribly burdensome, then it is not necessarily so. For here Levinas, with considerable acuity, sees that there is a kind of freedom in this idea of infinite responsibility. In my encounter with the other person, I am freed for a moment from my self-concern, from the dreariness of the same old thing to which I am accustomed. This may be, as Levinas claims, a 'difficult' freedom: it is certainly not the kind of freedom in which I am free as a bird, without responsibilities. But it is a kind of freedom all the same. The task of ethics, then, is unending; but because it is unending, there is always a possibility of freeing ourselves once again from the limiting self-concern into which we all, inevitably, fall. Here, I can do no better than quote the Talmudic passage with which Levinas himself was familiar:

> Rabbi Tarfon used to say: The day is short, the work is great; the workers are lazy, the reward is great, and the master is insistent. He also used to say: You are not called to complete the work, nor are you free to evade it. (Gibbs 2000, 383)

Ethically speaking, we are all incorrigible shirkers. When called upon to respond, we often walk past, as I walked on past the man in the marketplace in Darjeeling. But the demand does not go away. It is something with which we are continually presented in our relationships with others. Even if we do not have to save the world or complete the work, we are never free of the demand to respond. And when we do respond, there's no telling where we might end up. When you think about it—when you *really* think about it—it is frightening.

Ethics for the Overwrought

I have attempted here to give a rough outline of Levinas's phenomenology of one particular kind of ethical experience—the encounter with the face of another—to suggest how Levinas may have succeeded in capturing something of the 'what is it like?' of our face-to-face encounters with each other. But the stories that Levinas tells are rather more complicated and interesting than may seem to be the case from the account given above. If we are to understand Levinas as a storyteller of ethics—and if we are to open up some space for other, different stories—then we need to understand in a little more detail precisely what kind of storyteller Levinas is.[7]

It becomes apparent very early on that Levinas is at heart a tragedian. In the early part of *Totality and Infinity*, Levinas writes that his subject matter is the self, which he aims to explore as 'time, drama in several acts' (Levinas 1969, 24), but these acts are set against a remarkably dark backdrop. As Nietzsche once wrote, tragedy takes place against a dark background arising out of the 'terrible depths of nature' (Nietzsche 1993, 46): in other words, what makes a tragedy really tragic is not just that it is a series of unfortunate events, but also the faintly paranoid suspicion that the tragic nature of the universe as a whole is somehow conspiring in the unfolding of these events. The backdrop against which Levinas sets his own drama is explored in his book *Existence and Existents*, a book profoundly marked by the horror of his wartime internment. There he writes that, 'Existence of itself harbours something tragic which is not only there because of its finitude. Something that death cannot resolve' (Levinas 2001a, 5), and he goes on to write of the 'underlying tragic element in the ego, the fact that it is riveted to its own being' (Levinas 2001a, 84), and of the 'tragic involved in being' (Levinas 2001a, 87). As a phenomenologist, however, Levinas needs to provide some kind of demonstration of the tragedy that he sees as being involved in our existence. To this end, he proposes a thought-experiment to help us on our way.

> Let us imagine all beings, things and persons, reverting to nothingness. One cannot put this return to nothingness outside of all events. But what of this nothingness itself? Something would happen, if only night and the silence of nothingness... This impersonal, anonymous, yet inextinguishable 'consummation' of being, which murmurs in the depths of nothingness we shall designate by the term *there is*. The *there is*, inasmuch as it resists a personal form, is 'being in general'. (Levinas 2001a, 51-2)

In this book, Levinas explores a number of experiences— the rumbling and fitful insomnia when we are caught between sleep and wakefulness, the fatigue in which the shovel slips from the hand that grasps it—and weaves them together to tell a tragic story about existence in general. Caught between sleep and wakefulness, tossing fitfully in our beds, we cannot manage either to fully assume our existence, or to sink into blissful sleep; trapped between the demands of work and the body's fatigued resistance after a long day of physical labour, the hand feebly grips at the shovel even as the tool slips out of the grasp. In such experiences Levinas wants to persuade us that we are glimpsing something fundamental about what it is to exist: we are no longer ourselves, we are reduced to a kind of bare and claustrophobic existence from which there is no escape, and we see that existence itself simply rumbles onwards, interminable and anonymous. This, Levinas claims, is the background to our lives; and if we are to break with this anonymity, it is necessary to take a stand, the way that the tragic hero takes a stand—once again, the image comes from Nietzsche—as a 'light-image cast on a dark screen' (Nietzsche 1993, 46). Even to stand here and say 'I am!', Levinas tells us, is an act born out of 'My mastery, my virility, my heroism as a subject' (Levinas 2001, 72).

With the appearance of the tragic hero on the dark and gloomy stage, Levinas's drama can now move on. The elements rage around the hero, who rises up in the heart of all this turbulence and who begins to refashion the world. Through labour, the anonymous world becomes *my* world: 'a field cultivated by me, the sea in which I fish and moor my boats, the forest in which I cut wood' (Levinas 1969, 131); and through this labour, there is the possibility of opening up a space for reflection and peace (Levinas 2001a, 96). The tragedy that Levinas is weaving now begins to metamorphose into something else, almost into a kind of idyll in which I find that I am at home in the world, in which there is the possibility of peace and of enjoyment. Life, fortunately, is not just stark heroism, but it is also the 'love of life' (Levinas 1969, 145). Here we might imagine the image of the hero of Levinas's drama—having tamed the woodlands and tilled the fields, having erected sturdy walls to keep the elements at bay—finally at home with himself (and, because Levinas's storytelling is strongly gendered, it always is *himself*), contented, puffing on a pipe as he listens to the whistling wind outside. And yet our hero's contentment, happiness and love of life can never be complete. As in William Stafford's poem, 'Fall Wind', the walls are thin, and the rumbling anonymity of the world is not overcome, but is merely held in abeyance:

> *Pods of summer crowd around the door; I take them*
> *in the autumn of my hands.*
>
> *Last night I heard the first cold wind outside; The*
> *wind blew soft, and yet I shiver twice:*
>
> *Once for thin walls, once for the sound of time.*
> *(Stafford 1997, 75)*

Now the drama moves on once again as the idyll is eroticised. We see the hero returning from his labours to enjoy the pleasures of the silent, unspeaking caress of the 'feminine other', as the wind murmurs around the walls of his house (Levinas 1969, 155). At this point, many readers of Levinas may (and many indeed do) baulk at the decidedly patriarchal nature of the story that is being played out—this is something that I have discussed at greater length elsewhere (Buckingham 2013); but if we can put to one side for a moment these legitimate objections to the tale that Levinas is unfolding, it is possible at least to see that he recognises there are more aspects to the phenomenology of our relationships with others than is suggested by the account he gives of the face alone. Others, that is to say, are not just strangers for whom we are responsible, but they can also be friends, companions, lovers, members of the same family, or those with whom we find ourselves in community; and any account of ethics must—as we will see later—take note of many kinds of otherness.[8]

It is the stranger, however, who brings something so wholly new and unexpected that it breaks entirely with the world that we experience. How many stories begin with a knock on the door, with the arrival of the stranger who is strange not only in the sense of being unknown to the protagonist but also in a deeper, more unsettling sense? Our encounter with the face of the other, Levinas argues, is an encounter with this fundamental strangeness. The moment the door opens, and we see a stranger standing on the threshold, suddenly everything is at stake. We know from the stories that the stranger could be anyone at all: a god in disguise; a long lost brother or sister; an old enemy bent on revenge; a future friend or lover; even Death itself, inviting us to a final game of chess... And so the idea of the face enters Levinas's drama as an infinite strangeness, and in the process changes the story from a temporary idyll (idylls, after all, never last) to a kind of quest in which we find ourselves setting our course 'for a land not of our birth, for a land foreign to every nature, which has not been our fatherland and to which we shall never betake ourselves' (Levinas 1969, 34). Because of its infinite scope, and because the object towards which we are moving is something that we can never grasp—like the Grail in the myths, or like the famous crock of gold at the end of the rainbow—this might be called a metaphysical quest. As Barber notes in his study of Grail myths in European culture, 'the Grail functions ultimately as something beyond the reach of the ordinary world' (Barber 2004, 5). Yet there is something glorious in this risk and in this quest for the unattainable land to which we shall never betake ourselves, or for the unattainable cup that we will never hold in our hands. As we step beyond the threshold, we are for a moment freed from the rumbling horror that underlies existence. The stranger, Levinas says, 'opens time' for me (Levinas 2006, 225), offering me a future that I could not possibly have chosen for myself. I am not thereby wholly liberated from the tragedy that runs through existence, but a little space is opened up so that the tragedy loses its grip on me, so that it loses a little of its sting.[9]

As a drama in several acts, this is no doubt compelling in its own way; but it is tempting to ask what stories have been left out of Levinas's 'subtle interweaving of narrative and argument' (MacDonald 2005, 183).[10] For all of Levinas's astute phenomenological insights, it might well seem that this is far from being the only story possible—and that perhaps it is far from being the best. What other stories, it is tempting to ask, might we spin alongside those that are spun by Levinas himself?

In asking this question, we find ourselves having to address a puzzling feature of Levinas's work, because if we have been considering Levinas here as a storyteller of ethics, it has to be said that—like Plato before him—he is a remarkably reluctant one. Levinas may be a storyteller, but he is a storyteller who mistrusts the telling of stories, a hydrophobic sailor on the sea of stories.[11] It may be on account of this mistrust that, although he admits to being moved by Rosenzweig's criticisms of the philosophical tradition in the West, he nevertheless says next to nothing about Rosenzweig's suggestion that storytelling might be a suitable method for philosophy to follow. The question we must ask here is this: *why not?*

Overcoming Hydrophobia

Hydrophobia of this kind has a long history in the West, and if we are to really take storytelling seriously as a method, then it will be useful to lay these hydrophobic fears to rest. The objections that Levinas advances against storytelling—and also against other forms of representation—echo objections that have been bobbing around on the ocean ever since the days of Plato. Broadly speaking, these objections are twofold. Firstly, that stories risk fixing others within overarching systems of thought that lead almost inevitably to a kind of inhumanity. I tell a story about you, and in telling a story, I trap you in a system of my own making, a system in which there is no breathing-space, in which you have no voice of your own. Through telling tales (the story goes) we seek to master others, to control them, to gain dominion over them. And secondly, the very power to enchant that draws us to stories may itself be something to be feared. Stories are capable of stripping us of our sober reasoning, of leading us into states in which we are no longer in our right minds. They can, quite literally, take possession of us.

Levinas himself touches on these concerns, although in the broader context of representation in general, in his essay, 'Reality and Its Shadow'. In this early essay, he writes that art,

> brings into the world the obscurity of fate, but it especially brings the *ir*responsibility that charms as lightness and as grace. It frees. To make or to appreciate a novel and a picture is to no longer have to conceive, it is to renounce the effort of science, philosophy and action. Do not speak, do not reflect, admire in silence and in peace—such are the counsels of wisdom satisfied before the beautiful. Magic, recognised everywhere as the devil's, enjoys an incomprehensible tolerance in poetry. (Levinas 1998a, 12)

This is a peculiar passage. Why should Levinas oppose artistic representation to philosophy and action in this way? Why irresponsibility? And why this reference to *magic*, particularly as Levinas begins his essay by insisting that he is not just attempting to weave his own net of enchantment over the reader, but that he is instead attempting to move towards a greater degree of philosophical precision.[12]

To help us answer these questions, we can summon up three women who know a thing or two about magic: the witches from Macbeth. Their famous spell, 'Double, double toil and trouble...' admirably sums up Levinas's double unease. For, as Plato pointed out long ago, art endlessly reduplicates things ('double, double...'), producing copies and copies of copies and copies of copies of copies. Marina Warner—herself a storyteller of substantial talent—writes that, 'Representation itself acts as a form of doubling; representation exists in magical relation to the apprehensible world, it can exercise the power to make something come alive, *apparently*' (Warner 2004, 165). And once the thing represented has become alive (or at least *apparently*), it can exert a power over us. The traditional Western critique of idolatry—and when we are talking about the fear of stories, we are talking about representations, and thus cannot ignore the question of idolatry—has not been that idols are empty and without power. Instead, this fear is born out of the recognition that idols *are* powerful, that they are images with the power to enchant and fascinate, capable of bringing us under their sway. Why else put out the eyes of images, as the iconoclasts do?[13] Warner continues as follows:

> In one obvious sense, devils can only ever be 'painted devils', that is counterfeit, since they assume the forms they do in order to manifest themselves to humans. In the literature of doppelgängers, this question of the status of the double—is it real, or is it imagined?—and, if it is imagined, is it no less real for that?—returns insistently, and its undecidability, which gives many of its vehicles their narrative grip, finds expression through images of projections and images, artefacts and delusions and tries to decide their status with regard to the real. (Warner 2004, 167)

Representations are magical, and powerful, precisely because they inhabit this position of undecidability; and so the making of representations 'forms the chief basis of casting spells in medieval sorcery, as well as in the conjurer's and healers' arts with figures and *zemis* met with in the Americas' (Warner 2004, 168). While representations exert power over us, we cannot act upon them in turn: a painted apple can cause us to salivate, but we cannot take the apple that is represented, chop it up and make a pie out of it. 'An image,' Levinas writes, 'marks a hold of us rather than our initiative, a fundamental passivity' (Levinas 1998a, 3). This hold that images can exert over us is, however, something that can never bring us anything new. The artwork is frozen in time: the muscles of Laocoön and his sons in the famous sculpture are caught up in the grip of writhing serpents and are always straining towards a victory or a defeat that they will never attain. Mona Lisa's smile is suspended, either perpetually on the brink of breaking out into a full grin, or in the instant before it disappears altogether. The artwork may aspire to life, and yet the life it has is unfulfilled. According to Vasari, Donatello, carving in his studio, muttered to one of his creations 'Speak, damn you, speak!'—and yet the statue remained mute (Vasari 1987, 178). Evil powers, Levinas fears, 'are conjured by filling the world with idols which have mouths but do not speak' (Levinas 1998a, 12). However, Levinas does not stop here, for he also dreads the lulling of the wind and the waves, the delicious sleep that comes as the storyteller intones, the stilling of the heart and the mind through rhythm and through incantation. 'In rhythm,' he writes, 'there is no longer a oneself, but rather a sort of passage from oneself to anonymity. This is the captivation or incantation of poetry and music' (Levinas 1998a, 4). In poetry, we encounter 'a unique situation where we cannot speak of consent, assumption, initiative or freedom, because the subject is caught up and carried away by it' (Levinas 1998a, 4). To return to that spell from Shakespeare, we only have to think of the delicious rhythm of that line, a rhythm that has made it one of the most famous lines in all of English literature, to see with what supreme elegance Shakespeare blends the doubling and incantatory powers essential to the casting of spells.

In the face of all these lures and enchantments, Levinas puts forward a striking apology for charmless philosophical language. 'To poetic activity...' he writes, 'is opposed the language that at each instant dispels the charm of rhythm and prevents the initiative from becoming a role. Discourse (questioning and answering) is rupture and commencement, breaking of rhythm which enraptures and transports the interlocutors—prose' (Levinas 1969, 203).

And yet, for all of this, Levinas seems to find it hard to resist the lure of the sea. Not only is his work full of references to poets and storytellers—Aristophanes, Shakespeare, Homer, Dostoevsky, Euripides, Tolstoy, Rimbaud, Baudelaire and Goncharov all make an appearances—but as we have seen, his own work looks suspiciously like a kind of storytelling.[14] It is as if, in choosing ethics as one of his themes, Levinas has little choice but to have recourse to storytelling, that however much he may fear the sea, he cannot do without it if he wants to say anything at all.

It should be said that Levinas's fears are not entirely unreasonable. There is indeed something terrible in what Bruner refers to as 'the tyranny of a single story' (Bruner 2003, 103). To be trapped within a single tale removes the possibility of freedom. As Serres writes, 'as judicious as an idea appears to be, it becomes atrocious when it reigns alone' (Serres 1997, 122). Single stories, or closed systems of stories, are almost always tyrannical, which is why those such as Salman Rushdie—for whom stories are an unbounded, swelling sea—are frequently the subject of the ire of tyrants. In the light of Levinas's own wartime experiences, this queasiness with the way that tyrannical regimes sustain themselves by means of monomyths is both understandable and justified. Yet, while he resists single tales, Levinas shrinks back from the sheer profusion of stories that are possible, and the tales he tells take place within a remarkably narrow range. On those few occasions that Levinas dips his toes into the waters that lie beyond the relatively narrow compass of European thought with its dual heritage— the Greek and the Judaic—his fears turn positively lurid. 'The yellow peril!' he gasps in his essay *Le Débat Russo-Chinois et la Dialéctique*, 'It is not racial, it is spiritual. It does not involve inferior values; it involves a radical strangeness, a stranger to the weight of its past, from which there does not filter any familiar voice or inflection, a lunar or Martian past'—a passage that prompted Alford, in his essay on Levinas and politics, to ask in astonishment, 'Is Levinas out of his mind?' (Alford 2004, 160).[15]

Part of the difficulty that Levinas has is that he is working within a tradition that tends to see stories in isolation, that fails to recognise the fact that, as Roberto Calasso writes, 'Stories never live alone: they are branches of a family that we have to trace back, and forward' (Calasso 1994, 11). This is a tradition that goes all the way back to Aristotle who, for all of his insight, tended to see stories as self-contained entities. In his *Poetics*, Aristotle wrote of the tragic story as 'an imitation of an action that is complete in itself, as a whole of some magnitude', and he went on as follows:

> Now a whole is that which has beginning, middle, and end. A beginning is that which is not itself necessarily after anything else, and which has naturally something else after it; and end is that which is naturally after something itself, either as its necessary or usual consequent, and with nothing else after it; and a middle, that which is by nature after one thing and also another after it. (1450b)

In this view, the story—or at least the tragic story—does not follow from anything else in the world. It sustains itself by virtue of its own internal logic. When it ends, it ends without leaving a trace.[16] This is a strange idea. What event in the world, after all, does not follow from any other? What event has absolutely no consequences? If nothing else, we could say that a story might follow from the demand, 'Tell me a story!' And we might also admit that following on from the story, once we are tucked up in our bed and peacefully sleeping, the story might have further consequences in seeding dreams or nightmares. But in defining a story as a whole in this way, Aristotle tends to coil stories back in upon themselves, to isolate them from other times and other stories, to deny the kinship of which Calasso writes. It may, of course, be true that when we are *within* any particular tale, it may have to it an *appearance* of necessity, as if this story simply *had to* be. If the story is powerful and compelling enough, it can seem as if this story was there somewhere waiting to be written; it can even seem as if this one story's existence somehow refutes the existence of all other stories. This, however, is only from the perspective of standing *within* the story. Not only this, this is only from the perspective of standing within one particular kind of story. For if stories that are told in the West may, at certain times and in certain places, appear to a kind of self-containment, this is not the case elsewhere. For example, Somadeva's *Kathasaritsagara* displays a distinctly unaristotelian tendency to nest and frame stories, so that it is hard to tell where each begins and ends, a tendency that is even more pronounced in the *Yogavasishtha*, another Kashmiri text dating from between the tenth and twelfth centuries. The *Yogavasishtha* presents itself as a scripture written in stories. And as the scripture unfolds, it becomes clear that we are far from the kind of territory envisaged by Aristotle. Indeed, as Wendy Doniger notes, this particular text of nested narratives leaves us without any sense of solid ground at all.

> The *Yogavasishtha* is a story within a story... The very first verses of the *Yogavasishtha* tell us that the sage Agastya told Sutikshna about a Brahmin named Karunya, the son of Agnivesya, to whom Agnivesya told the story of a nymph named Suruci, who learned from a messenger of Indra that

the sage Valmiki had told Bharadvaja the story of how Rama
had heard from the sage Vasishtha a lot of stories... the stories
of this text. (O'Flaherty 1986, 240)

As the *Yogavasishtha* continues, the nesting becomes ever
more complex, so that by the time you have read only a few
pages, it is impossible to map precisely where one is within the
endless mass of stories, where one story begins and where
another one ends.

The various levels of dream, illusion and reality throughout
the text are continually confounded, time stretches and
compresses, whole universes are fitted into single moments or
moments are stretched to near eternity. In a story such as this,
there is nowhere for the Aristotelian theorist to get a foothold.
As Calasso once again notes—this time in his book on the
myths of India, a book that owes a great deal to the *Yogavasishtha*—'The beginning: something not to be found in nature'
(Calasso 1999, 399).

Neither in the story nor in nature is there any moment of
absolute beginning. Nor is there any moment of absolute
ending as the stories of the *Yogavasistha* and the *Kathasaritsagara* give rise to still further stories, stretching on endlessly
towards the horizon.

Thus, while the individual stories may claim special status
for themselves, there are always inevitably alternative versions,
variants, retellings that are subtly or radically different that can
call this special status into question. The Old Testament tale of
Noah is kin with the Sumerian tale of Atarhasis—a flood tale in
which the gods are multiple, not single—and these two are
avatars of the tale of Utnapishtim in the epic of Gilgamesh.
Rushdie knows this very well, and with a sly wink, he introduces a classification system for stories so bureaucratically
baroque that it becomes clear that it tends towards infinity.

What Haroun was experiencing, although he didn't know it, was Princess Rescue Story Number S/1001/ZHT/420/41(r)xi; and because the princess in this particular story had recently had a haircut and therefore had no long tresses to let down (unlike the heroine of Princess Rescue Story G/1001/RIM/777/M(w)I, better known as 'Rapunzel'), Haroun as the hero was required to climb up the outside of the tower by clinging to the cracks between the stones with his bare hands and feet. (Rushdie 1990, 71-2)

In recognising that stories are plural and that they are social beings by nature, it is possible to find an answer to Levinas's hydrophobia. When Cézanne repeatedly paints Mont Saint-Victoire, or when Hokusai returns again and again to paint Mount Fuji, instead of obscuring the things they paint, they could be said to bring us a renewed attentiveness—because painters are phenomenologists too—to the things themselves. If I were to travel to Japan and stand before Mount Fuji, I would do so not with an attentiveness born of bare seeing, but with an attentiveness made keen by my love of Hokusai's prints. I would see the mountain with the care and the love that comes from knowing it is precisely *this* mountain, and not some other, before which I stand. Similarly, if I allow many stories to be told, then storytelling too can bring us to a new attentiveness. The problem does not lie in our desire to represent the world, but in our insistence that this, and only this, representation is the true representation. Mount Fuji lives for us from and through the endless representations that have been made of it, not simply as a sign amongst signs, as the semioticians might have it, not as just one node in the semiotic thicket, but as a *mountain*; and not just as any old mountain, but as *this* mountain.

If one resists the lure of any single tale, then it becomes possible to recognise that there are many kinds of poetic enchantment. For every siren who sings to make us forget, only to draw us to our deaths upon the rocks, there are perhaps a hundred other singers who ease the heart: the hum of crickets on a summer's night, the storyteller who stands by the fire and whose voice allows us to forget the petty trivia of our daily concerns, the soft and comforting words of a friend that ease the burden of our grief. 'One must not sleep,' Levinas writes, 'One must philosophise' (Levinas 1998b, 15). But it is also true that, at times, one must not philosophise: one must sleep. And here, perhaps, there is no better way of calming the hydrophobic fears we may have of the multiplication of images and the lulling rhythms of the sea than by recourse to the words of Gaston Bachelard as he drifts off to sleep to the everyday sounds of the traffic passing through the streets of Paris.

> We all know that the big city is a clamorous sea, and it has been said countless times that, in the heart of night in Paris, one hears the ceaseless murmur of flood and tide. So I make a sincere image out of these hackneyed ones, an image that is as much my own as though I myself had invented it, in line with my gentle mania for always believing that I am subject of what I am thinking. If the hum of cars becomes more painful, I do my best to discover in it the roll of thunder, of a thunder that speaks to me and scolds me. And I feel sorry for myself. So there you are, unhappy philosopher, caught up again by the storm, by the storms of life! I dream an abstract-concrete daydream. My bed is a small boat lost at sea; that sudden whistling is the wind in the sails. On every side the air is filled with the sound of furious klaxoning. I talk to myself to give myself cheer: there now, your skiff is holding its own, you are safe in your stone boat. Sleep, in spite of the storm. Sleep in the storm. Sleep in your own courage, happy to be a man who is assailed by the

wind and wave. And I fall asleep, lulled by the noise of Paris. (Bachelard 1992, 28)[17]

The Varieties of Ethical Experience

The tales that Levinas weaves in *Totality and Infinity* have an undeniable power. But once we have started to overcome our hydrophobic fears of the ocean, it is hard not to wonder whether these stories, for all of their power, are the only stories possible. To be sure, we need not dismiss his phenomenological data: at times it may seem as if the world does present us with a 'moiling darkness'; the freedom that we experience in responding to another person can seem to us to be a 'difficult' freedom, and so on. Yet there are many kinds of stories, and many kinds of experiences, that do not appear in Levinas's tragic drama. Let us take two examples. The first example is a very different account of the encounter with that which Levinas sees as the rumbling anonymity of existence. Does the break-up of a sense of self (a sense of self that, as Rosenzweig has pointed out, may not be as fundamental to everyday experience as we once might have thought) need to be a return to a kind of horror, or can it be something more joyful? Here is the thirteenth-century Japanese thinker Dogen, exploring the loss of self-identity, but without any suggestion of the tragic weight of which Levinas writes:

> To study the Way is to study the self. To study the self is to forget the self. To forget the self is to be enlightened by all things of the universe. (Kim and Leighton 2004, 104)

Kopf points out in his study of Dogen and phenomenology that the Japanese thinker explicitly links the alienation that comes from an attempt to separate ourselves from the world with a form of delusion (Kopf 2001). This is a delusion not only about the world but also about ourselves; and with this delusion comes a kind of bondage. To study the self, on the other hand, is to recognise that this self that we imagine to be separate is, in fact, a part of the world. In recognising this, there is indeed a return to a kind of anonymous existence. This return, however, is not to be feared. Instead, it has about it a taste of an exhilarating, if bracing, freedom. Dogen captures something of this taste when he asks, in his *Eihei Koroku*, 'Unless the cold pierces through our bones once, how can we have the apricot blossoms perfuming the whole world?' (Cleary 1992, 53).

The second example comes from another Buddhist source, but one that is far distant from Dogen. The eighth-century Indian philosopher-monk Shantideva acknowledged, as did Levinas much later, that the demands of ethics were in fact infinite. And yet he did so in a very different emotional register, suggesting that we might respond to this infinite demand with all of the light-hearted joy of an elephant leaping in the heat of the day from cooling lotus pool to cooling lotus pool (Shantideva 1998).

These counter-examples suggest that the tragic tale woven by Levinas is far from being the only tale we could tell, and that it is not necessarily called forth by the phenomenological data. When all is said and done, it is not philosophically more correct to rise up in the morning with a sick and heavy heart than it is to leap out of bed with alacrity and delight.[18] The drama that Levinas has chosen to unfold, although it may be internally coherent, and although it has an undeniable power of its own, is only one possible drama. There is indeed, Hilary Putnam points out in his essay on Levinas, no single *sine qua non* to the ethical life (Putnam 2002, 57); and seeing Levinas's drama as precisely this—a drama, a loosely-woven tapestry of stories—allows us to permit that there are many other possible dramas and stories, dramas and stories to which Levinas pays little heed.

In the chapters that follow, then, I want to allow back in some of the kinds of stories that Levinas excludes. This might not only have the effect of opening up a broader understanding of ethics than Levinas permits, but it might also give us a way of thinking through Levinas's genuinely useful phenomenological insights into the 'what is it like?' of ethics, without feeling that we are thereby committed to the tragic drama that he weaves. It is time, in other words, to cast off into strange new territories in the company of even stranger companions—gods who steal from human beings, talking fish, desert travellers, and eccentric sages—to see where we end up.

6

STORIES ABOUT STORIES

L et us set out, then, by telling stories about the telling of stories, stories in which storytelling itself is at issue.[1] As Benjamin notes, there are two tribes of storytellers, although these tribes are not absolutely distinct and tend to 'overlap in many ways' (Benjamin 2006, 144). The first are those who come from afar, the travellers across foreign seas; the second are those who stay at home and 'make an honest living.' Given that we are still novice navigators, we will begin with a story that is—at least in terms of the Western philosophical tradition—somewhat closer to home. Only after this will we join the other tribe of storytellers and set off for more distant parts of the ocean.

The Shudder of Thought

Our first tale will come from the opening sections of Kierkegaard's book *Fear and Trembling*, published under the pseudonym Johannes de Silentio. The prelude of Kierkegaard's book begins with the following words: 'There was once a man...' With this beginning, we sense that here is a philosopher who knows how to tell a good story.

> He had learned as a child that beautiful tale of how God tried Abraham, how he withstood the test, kept his faith and for the second time received a son against every expectation. (Kierkegaard 1985, 44)

The book has only just begun, and we are already dealing not just with stories, but with stories about stories. Kierkegaard assumes that his readers know the original to which he is referring; but those of us who read him today may find that—just to remind ourselves—we need to turn aside for a few moments and track down the source text in Genesis 22, where it goes like this:

> And it came to pass after these things, that God did tempt Abraham, and said unto him, Abraham: and he said, Behold, here I am.
>
> And he said, Take now thy son, thine only son Isaac, whom thou lovest, and get thee into the land of Moriah; and offer him there for a burnt offering upon one of the mountains which I will tell thee of.
>
> And Abraham rose up early in the morning, and saddled his ass, and took two of his young men with him, and Isaac his son, and clave the wood for the burnt offering, and rose up, and went unto the place of which God had told him.
>
> Then on the third day, Abraham lifted up his eyes, and saw the place afar off.
>
> And Abraham said unto his young men, Abide ye here with the ass; and I and the lad will go yonder and worship, and come again to you.
>
> And Abraham took the wood of the burnt offering, and

laid it upon Isaac his son; and he took the fire in his hand, and a knife; and they went both of them together.

And Isaac spake unto Abraham his father, and said, My father: and he said, Here am I, my son. And he said, Behold the fire and the wood: but where is the lamb for a burnt offering?

And Abraham said, My son, God will provide himself a lamb for a burnt offering: so they went both of them together.

And they came to the place which God had told him of; and Abraham built an altar there, and laid the wood in order, and bound Isaac his son, and laid him on the altar upon the wood.

And Abraham stretched forth his hand, and took the knife to slay his son.

And the angel of the LORD called unto him out of heaven, and said, Abraham, Abraham: and he said, Here am I.

And he said, Lay not thine hand upon the lad, neither do thou any thing unto him: for now I know that thou fearest God, seeing thou hast not withheld thy son, thine only son from me.

And Abraham lifted up his eyes, and looked, and behold behind him a ram caught in a thicket by his horns: and Abraham went and took the ram, and offered him up for a burnt offering in the stead of his son.

What, in heaven's name, are we to make of this strange and barbaric tale? How is it to be interpreted? What does it *mean*? The starkness and the violence, the baffling commands from on high, the strange calm of Abraham as he prepares for the sacrifice: none of these allow us easily to get a foothold in the story, or suggest a clear and unambiguous interpretation. But this, it becomes clear, is precisely why Kierkegaard is so fascinated by the story. As with the *Yogavasishtha*, no sooner have we begun to read then we find ourselves not just dealing with a story (the story of Abraham and Isaac), nor with a story within a story (the story of a man who is reading the story about Abraham and Isaac), but with a story within a story within a story (the story of Johannes de Silentio who is telling us a story about a man who is reading about Abraham and Isaac). Incidentally, the dizziness does not stop here, for as I write this, I find myself in turn telling a story about how Kierkegaard is telling a story about how Johannes de Silentio is telling a story...[2] And if this was not enough, the story that lurks at the heart of this nesting of tales is itself profoundly perplexing. Kierkegaard has de Silentio write how, as the reader of the story of Abraham and Isaac became older,

> he read the same story with even greater admiration, for life had divided what had been united in the child's pious simplicity. The older he became the more often his thoughts turned to that tale, his enthusiasm became stronger and stronger, and yet less and less could he understand it. Finally it put everything else out of his mind; his soul had but one wish, actually to see Abraham, and one longing, to have been witness to those events. (Kierkegaard 1985, 44).

Now the complications multiply still further, for as he explores this longing and this bafflement Kierkegaard (or Johannes?) sets out on a curious course: he tells—or retells—the story of Abraham and Isaac not once, but four times, each time differently. So now we have multiple tellings of the same, nested story, each telling throwing up new questions or casting new light on this ancient tale. In the first telling, Abraham tells his son that the sacrifice is not God's command, but that instead he, Abraham, is an idolater: he damns himself in his son's eyes so that his son does not turn away from God. The second telling takes place in grim silence, and Abraham does not speak either before, during or after the terrible events of the tale; but for the rest of his days, 'Abraham's eye was darkened, he saw joy no more' (Kierkegaard 1985, 46). The third telling begins as the second, but this time Abraham throws himself on his face, begging God to forgive him for his willingness to sacrifice his son. Then he spends the remainder of his days in solitude: here it is not so much the sacrifice as the solitary journeying of Abraham that becomes the main focus of the story, as Abraham rides more and more 'frequently on his lonely way', finding no peace in the world (Kierkegaard 1985, 47). Finally, in the last telling, Isaac himself is witness to the anguish that runs through Abraham as he goes about preparing the sacrifice with an air of apparent calm. But Abraham nevertheless draws the knife; and when Isaac sees this, and sees the shudder that runs through his father's body, the boy's faith crumbles.

Things are already looking tangled, but they become more tangled yet, because amongst these retellings, Kierkegaard interweaves another curious series of stories concerning the weaning of a child from the mother's breast. Hall writes that Kierkegaard 'has de Silentio bring Abraham's conundrum into the nursery' (Hall 2002, 71), arguing that by setting the two dramas—the drama of weaning and the drama in the story—alongside each other, Kierkegaard is drawing explicit parallels between the ordinariness of our everyday, domestic dramas and the seemingly impossible situation that Abraham faces. 'Our lives, and our daily loves, are somehow implicated through Abraham's singular task,' she writes. This may be so, but another reading is possible. Perhaps the imagery of weaning stands in direct relation to Kierkegaard's understanding of the nature of stories (such as this one) that resist all interpretation. Each attempt to retell the story in a way that makes sense of it is an attempt to return to the metaphorical breast of one comforting interpretation or another. By the time Kierkegaard has finished with us, it has become clear that we simply cannot interpret away the disturbing heart of this story, if we are still to give the story it's due. Perhaps Kierkegaard is himself attempting to wean us off the solid food of our calm interpretations and our unruffled certainties, so that we too might reach a point at which we cry out, along with the reader in the text, 'Yet no one was as great as Abraham; who is able to understand him?' (Kierkegaard 1985, 48).

This, it seems, is the heart of the fascination that this story holds for Kierkegaard: the story of Abraham and Isaac comprehensively resists any attempt to derive from it any obvious propositions or ethical maxims, while on the other hand, the intensity of the drama is such that it nevertheless demands our attention. In setting himself against any interpretive approaches to the story, Kierkegaard tells a caustic tale of a priest who preaches on Abraham and Isaac one Sunday, and who takes the story as an illustration of the commonplace proposition that Abraham's 'greatness was that he so loved God that he was willing to offer him the best he had' (Kierkegaard 1985, 58). Kierkegaard goes on to imagine a member of the congregation who, on hearing these words, comes to the 'most profound, tragic-comic misunderstanding.' The pious parishioner goes home wanting to do just like Abraham and, taking in his hand the carving knife that has been laid out for the Sunday roast, sets upon his own son in emulation of the Patriarch. Yet Kierkegaard reserves his condemnation and mockery not for the member of the congregation, but for the priest who, in repeating platitudes about the story without a hint of perspiration, 'hadn't known what he was saying' (Kierkegaard 1985, 59).

What the priest had missed, as far as Kierkegaard is concerned, was that the story is more than an illustration, that it is more than a well-crafted artefact. It is 'not the finely wrought fabric of imagination, but the shudder of thought' (Kierkegaard 1984, 44). This distinction is crucial. There is to a story—or at least to this story—more than the artfulness of its composition, the exoticism of the setting, the charm of the telling. A story is more than style and content, precisely because it is a *telling*, and in this telling, something may take place, a shuddering of the one who tells the story, or of the one to whom the story is told. The story of Abraham and Isaac, resisting all of our attempts at translation into 'morals', leaves us nothing to fall back upon except this shudder, nothing except the troubling nature of the story itself.[3]

Here, however, it may be that Kierkegaard fails to fully rise to the challenge that he himself has set. Seeing no hope of solid ground, in the 'Speech In Praise of Abraham' that follows on directly from the retellings of the story of Abraham and Isaac, he puts forward the following wager:

> If there were no eternal consciousness in a man, if at the bottom of everything there were only a wild ferment, a power that twisting in dark passions produced everything great or inconsequential; if an unfathomable, insatiable emptiness lay hid beneath everything, what would life be but despair? If it were thus, if there were no sacred bond uniting mankind, if one generation rose up after another like the leaves of the forest, if one generation succeeded the other as the songs of birds in the woods, if the human race passed through the world as a ship through the sea or the wind through the desert, a thoughtless and fruitless whim, if an eternal oblivion always lurked hungrily for its prey and there were no power strong enough to wrest it from its clutches—how empty and devoid of comfort life would be! But for that reason it is not so... (Kierkegaard 1985, 49)

Here we see the same kind of horror at existence that shudders through the very different tales that Levinas tells. And faced by this horror, Kierkegaard makes a desperate leap, retreating to an 'eternal consciousness' that might be able to snatch meaning from the meaninglessness of the world. But it is hard not to wonder whether this recourse to an idea of eternal consciousness somehow undermines the potency of the tale. The shudder of thought that we experience when we read a story such as this is a physical shudder, something that ripples through the body, the shaking of an organism whose thinking is never divorced from living flesh. This shudder is worth paying attention to, even if we do not join Kierkegaard in the leap that he makes, and even if we are sceptical of the high drama of eternal oblivion and insatiable emptiness. It may be true that the world is a sea through which we pass as ships, but if that is so, as we have already seen, hydrophobia will get us nowhere. Instead, it might be helpful to explore the 'twisting dark patterns' that menace us in nightmares, in the hope that, through a close attentiveness, they may lose their aura of dark horror and may reveal themselves as no more than the endlessly fascinating and subtle movements of the winds and the tides.

The tale of Abraham and Isaac is interesting because it gives us very little to hold on to. It does not resolve itself into any clear interpretations. As the interpretations we give to the story fall away one by one, we are left only with our bafflement and with the perpetual rising of goose-bumps on our flesh. But perhaps this story is not unique in its power to cause such a shuddering, for the shudder of thought may be simply a matter of the sensuality of the story, a reflection of the fact that stories are always embodied, the tales of Prince Red Peter and of Kikori and Fly no less than that of Abraham and Isaac. The horripilation that we might feel when we read the tale of Abraham and Isaac (or, for that matter, that tale of Prince Red Peter, or of Kikori and Fly) may perhaps seem remarkable; but it is also ordinary. Our speech, after all, is born in the body; the images we dream are bodily images. It would be astonishing if stories did not have this effect on us; it would be astonishing if we did not find ourselves shuddering with thought. Even the most rarefied philosophical reflection takes place here in the body. There is no thought that doesn't, in one way or another, cause us to shudder.[4] That words, mere words, could have the power to make the skin of the back fluctuate as if burned by some icy fire—a thought that shakes the creature who thinks it —can indeed seem miraculous; but it is only miraculous to those who have painstakingly and arbitrarily prised apart mind and body to conclude that this organism is double in nature, and who have then idled away endless hours in speculating about what glue could possibly be strong enough to rejoin the two severed parts. The famous claim that in the beginning there was the Word, and that the Word was then made flesh is, in the light of all available evidence, mistaken. As Varela points out, 'We reflect on a world that is not made, but found, and yet it is also our structure that enables us to reflect upon this world' (Varela 1993, 3). First the flesh, then the word: this is the true order of priority. Long ago, in warm primaeval seas that were without language, fleshy creatures, our ancestors, went about their business, creatures capable of shuddering and flinching. In the beginning was the Flesh. And the Flesh was made garrulous.[5]

On Speech, Writing and Stories

Here it is necessary to deal with a distinction that is often made within the philosophy of language: the distinction between speech and writing. For if I am talking about stories, it might be asked whether I am talking only about oral storytelling, or whether what I am saying also applies to the written word. And we might be tempted to claim that while language is clearly embodied, when we are dealing with the spoken word, when we turn our attention to the written word, this embodiment is far less certain. Not only this, but we might wonder whether there is a substantial difference between the kinds of thinking that take place in largely oral cultures, and the kinds of thinking that take place in cultures of the written word.[6] This raises philosophical issues that date back at least as far as Plato's *Phaedrus*, in which Plato tells the story of Socrates telling the story of how the god Theuth came to exhibit the arts he had invented to the king of all Egypt, Thamus.

> The story goes that Thamus said much to Theuth, both for and against each art. But when they came to writing, Theuth said: 'O King, here is something that, once learned, will make the Egyptians wiser and will improve their memory; I have discovered a potion for memory and for wisdom.' Thamus, however, replied, 'O most expert Theuth, one man can give birth to the elements of an art, but only another can judge how they can benefit or harm those who will use them. And now, since you are the father of writing, your affection for it has made you describe its effects as the opposite of what they really are. In fact, it will introduce forgetfulness into the soul of those who learn it: they will not practice using their memory because they will put their trust in writing, which is external and depends on signs that belong to others, instead of trying to remember from the inside, completely on their own. You have not discovered a potion for remembering, but for reminding; you provide your students with the appearance of wisdom, not with its reality.' (274e-275a)

Socrates goes on to claim—at least, according to Plato—that, 'When it has once been written down, every discourse roams about everywhere, reaching indiscriminately those with understanding no less than those who have no business with it, and it doesn't know to whom it should speak and to whom it should not,' contrasting this with the 'living, breathing discourse of the man who knows, of which the written one can be fairly called an image.' There are three distinct claims here. The first is that the written word does not serve memory but instead that it serves forgetting; the second is that the written word is not directed towards what Rosenzweig would call a 'particular someone,' but towards anyone or no-one; and the third is that the written word is, in a sense, dead: it does not live and breathe, but is merely an image of that which truly lives. In this way, Plato salvages some place for philosophical writing, saying that philosophical writing can act not to teach us new knowledge, but as 'reminders for those who already know.' This, however, is as far as Plato will go.

While it may well be that writing, in one sense, serves not memory but forgetting, that is not our concern at the moment.[7] It may also be that the written word does not address itself to the individual as the spoken word does. Again, this is not of immediate import here. What is of interest, however, is Plato's claim that the written word is not a 'living, breathing' discourse. In one sense, Plato is entirely correct. If I receive a letter from a friend, while it lies on the doormat, it does not live and breathe. But when my friend wrote the letter, or when I come to read it, at these times it is a different matter: there is a liveliness to reading and a liveliness to writing. Questions of memory on one side, despite all differences between written and spoken forms, both are nevertheless manifestations of language; and writing and reading are, like speaking and listening, the activities of an embodied, living, breathing, person.[8] The writer and the reader, too, are capable of shuddering. If certain philosophers have disparaged the written word and claimed that true philosophy must happen in spoken communication, so too have those writing on the subject of narrative tended to denigrate those stories that are written. Thus, although Niles aptly describes the human species as *Homo narrans*, he then goes on to claim that 'Oral narrative, or what we call storytelling in

everyday speech, is as much around us as the air we breathe...'
(Niles 1999, 1), thereby restricting storytelling to the spoken
word. Walter Benjamin, too, exhibits a kind of nostalgia for
spoken forms of narrative, claiming that, '... among those
writers who have set down the tales, the great ones are those
whose written version differs least from the speech of many
nameless storytellers' (Benjamin 2006, 146). For Benjamin, oral
storytelling—which has been supplanted by the novel—is true
storytelling; and, as for Plato, true knowledge is the knowledge
that I come to through my own reflection or thorough genuine
philosophical dialogue. For both thinkers, the written form is a
reminiscence, a trace or a reminder: for Plato a reminder of
what we already know, and in a more melancholy vein, for
Benjamin, a reminder of what we have lost for good.

Let us, however, step back a moment. Laying on one side
this often rather arid argument between the written and the
spoken word, we can see that as *Homo narrans* we are compul-
sive storytellers, and this compulsion takes shape in whatever
form is available to us: written language, spoken language,
semaphore. To be sure, speech—relying merely on our biological capacities and not on any other technologies—is in one
sense more fundamental than writing (or, for that matter,
semaphore) and it is also much more widespread. It is probably
the case that, unless we are scholar-hermits, we speak more
words than we write and we hear more words than we read.
Nevertheless, in the present context there is no need to draw
such firm distinctions between the written and the spoken.
After all, we can encounter what we might naïvely call the
same story both in written and spoken form.[9] Instead, we
might do better to see the various technologies of communication that human societies have developed as speech by other
means, each with their own advantages and limitations, rather
than as forms of language that are somehow opposed to
speech.[10]

The Trembling of the Flesh

When we allow ourselves to consider the embodiment of stories—whether spoken or written—then we open up a range of questions that go beyond questions of language and of interpretation; and here the seeming gap suggested by the philosopher Paul Ricoeur when he writes that 'stories are recounted, life is lived. An unbridgeable gap (which) seems to separate fiction and life' (Ricoeur 1991, 25) begins to close. Stories, after all, are not only recounted, but they, too, are lived.[11] From this viewpoint, Ricoeur—a thinker who is deeply indebted to the traditions of phenomenology—does not go far enough when he suggests that stories function as a way of experimenting with questions of real, live ethics:

> Literature is a vast laboratory in which we experiment with estimations, evaluations, and judgements of approval and condemnation through which narrativity serves as a propaedeutic to ethics. (Ricoeur 1994, 115)

Literature, of course, *may* be a way of experimenting with estimations, evaluations, judgements of approval and condemnation; but de Silentio's problem was that the story of Abraham and Isaac simply confounded *all* attempts at any such experimentation. We must return, therefore, to the shudder that escapes our attempts at interpretation. Kierkegaard's telling of stories about the telling of stories about the telling of stories is a way of bringing this shudder, so easily forgotten, to the forefront of our awareness. And we find that what goes on in the telling goes far beyond the sum of all possible interpretations, however subtle or illuminating these may be. The telling of a story does more than deliver us lucid meanings that can be expressed in the language of propositions and maxims. What is missing from such an account is the phenomenon of the story as a *telling*, the passage that I, a living creature of shuddering flesh, undergo—whether as a storyteller, or as the one who hears, or as the one who reads.

It is necessary, then, to return to the method of storytelling once again, in the hope that this might allow us to say something more about this kind of passage. The story we will consider here is one that has the virtue of being less discussed in the intellectual traditions of the West, and therefore less crowded with well-worn 'philosophical' interpretations. The story concerns King Sivi, a hawk and a dove.

This tale has lived through many retellings in India and beyond, and is usually identified as a Jataka tale, belonging to the collections of 'birth stories' of the Buddha and dating at least from early Buddhist times.[12] In the retelling that follows, I am relying heavily upon R. K. Narayan's translation, which has the strong advantage of making the same move that Kierkegaard makes in his *Fear and Trembling*: it introduces the teller of the tale into the fabric of the tale itself. Once more, we find ourselves telling stories about the telling of stories.

∼

Of Hawks and Doves

Let us imagine, then, that the scene is rural India. A storyteller —a wanderer with ragged clothing and a drum—has arrived in the village. He is an old man, and he carries the drum under his arm. He settles down at the foot of a tree, in a cool spot beside a stream on the margins of the village, he places the drum in his lap, and he begins to play.

Bdoumm! Bdoumm! Bdoumm!

At the sound of the Storyteller's drum the villagers begin to emerge from their houses, some curious and some affecting boredom. They stand around or settle on the ground, each one of them looking at the Storyteller and making their separate judgements: 'here is an old fool sent to try us'; 'here is a man who has come to fill our heads with nonsense'; 'here is a wise man, knowledgeable in the Vedas'; 'here is a man who belongs to the past, not the present': but although each one of them comes to his or her own opinion, nobody speaks.

The wood of the drum has been burnished to a shine where it has been held in the Storyteller's hand every day for the past fifty years. The skin, which was last replaced when he could still walk without stiffness, is thin to the point of being almost translucent. It will last him, may the gods help him, as long as he needs.

Bdoumm! Ta-ka-ta. Bdoumm! Ta-ka-ta. Bdoumm! Ta-ka-ta. Bdoumm!

The villagers cluster in a semicircle around the old man. One or two—back at home in the village for a few days, leaving behind their city lives—chew gum and affect looks of boredom, although even they found it impossible not to come to hear the teller when he arrived. Children sit at the front of the crowd, wide-eyed. The rhythms of the drum become more complex.

Bdoumm! Ta-ka-ta-Ta-ka-ta. Bdoumm! Ta-ka-ta-Ta- ka-ta. Bdoumm! Ta-ka-ta-Ta-ka-ta. Bdoumm!

Then the Storyteller opens his eyes. His teeth are missing: not once during his long life has he seen fit to visit the dentist. Dentists demand money, and the Storyteller has rarely even held a coin or a banknote in his hand, let alone had enough for dentures, fillings or root canal work.

'May Shiva, he of the blue throat, swallower of poison and saviour of the world, he who is caught in the silken noose of Parvati's amorous glances, grant you wealth and prosperity,' he begins, the words accompanied by a rippling of his old fingers on the drum-skin, but gently now: *Ta-ka-ta Ta-ka-ta-ta Ta-ka-ta-ka-ta.*

'And may Ganesha,' the Storyteller continues, 'who dances

at the fading of the day to brush away the old stars and who sprays the heavens anew with the milk of his trunk, protect you and bring you happiness. But may your own wisdom guide you.'

Ta-ka-ta Ta-ka-ta Ta Bdoumm!

The Storyteller places the drum on the ground beside him, looking around his audience. 'And may Vac,' he says, concluding his opening invocation, 'the goddess of speech who brings light to everything known and unknown, direct me in my telling.'

The Storyteller lowers his eyes, and he begins to speak of hawks and of doves.

'King Sivi,' he says, 'was seated in the shade of a tree, a tree so large and ancient that it could have been planted at the beginning of time itself. He was enjoying the cool afternoon shade and the relief that it offered after the furious heat of the day. As he gazed out over the lake, watching it shimmer in the haze, his brow unfolded itself and peace came into his heart. His mind, so long made small by the worries of a king—by the fear of murderers and of assassins, by fretful worrying over the future of the kingdom, by palace intrigues—became as still as a lake that perfectly reflects the orb of the full moon.

'Something heavy falling into the king's lap brought him back to his senses. King Sivi opened his eyes in surprise. He looked down and, before a thousand thoughts of murder and mutiny had the chance to crowd back into his mind, he saw a young dove in his lap, her feathers perfectly white, sprawling across his fine silk robes of red and gold. She was so exhausted that she could barely keep open a single pink eye and from her mouth came a feeble, fluttering cooing. The king gently picked her up and cradled her in his arms, soothing her as he had once soothed his son, waking from a nightmare, before the child had grown into the restless youth he now was. "My little one, what brings you to the lap of the king? What has caused you to fall from the sky like a stone? You are safe now, little one. There is nobody in this land more powerful than I. You will be protected from all dangers. Nothing can harm you now."

'At that moment there was cry from the heavens, and the king looked up. A tiny speck appeared in the sky, almost invisible against the sun. The king watched as the speck grew bigger, and as a hawk swooped down from an enormous height to hover just in front of his eyes. King and hawk looked at each other steadily. "O King!" cried the hawk, in such distress that tears were trickling from its eyes. "You must help me!"

The king had never seen a hawk weep before, for hawks weep only rarely and then almost always in private. "You are ruler of all in this country, and I ask for your mercy. I am hungry and have not eaten all day. That dove was to be my prey. Though it may pain you to do so, please give the dove to me so I do not starve." The hawk's feathered cheeks glistened with jewel-like tears.

'Instinctively the king wrapped the dove more closely inside his robe. The bird had begun to tremble in his arms, looking up at Sivi with eyes that were beyond weeping. The king looked down at the dove, feeling her warm, soft body shivering with fear. "King Sivi!" the dove cooed, her voice broken by terror. "I came to you for sanctuary, you who are my king and supreme protector. Do not hand me over, for I too fear death, I too feel pain."

'The king felt the weight of her tiny body in his robe, and he looked now at the dove, now at the hawk and now at the dove again. "Good king, you who are known throughout the world for your wisdom and your kindness," countered the hawk, "I have chased this dove all morning, and I have not the strength to chase another. I know that the dove feels pain, that it trembles before death and I am truly sorry; but I am a hawk, and it is my nature to chase doves for food. Though it may be hateful to me that I must live by the deaths of others, I cannot change my nature. Could I assume a diet of beans and of green plants, renouncing all living flesh, I assure you that I would do so; but I know of nobody who has discovered how to transform their nature to such an extent. If you do not hand over my prey, I shall starve. Have you no compassion?"

'King Sivi looked from one to the other. Then he reached into his robe, pulling out a knife with a long, curved blade of hammered gold—for a king always carries a knife underneath his robe, out of fear of rebellion, insurgency and parricide. He lifted the knife in the air and held it still for a moment, the curved blade, razor-sharp, an explosion of light in the afternoon sun.'

The Storyteller raises his hand in the air, and it is as if there is a knife held in that old fist.

'King Sivi plunged the blade,' he says, his voice so faint that the audience can barely make it out, bringing his hand down in a single, sweeping gesture, 'into the flesh of his very own thigh.'

A shudder passes through the audience. Several of them reach down involuntarily to touch their own thighs, as if they have felt for the briefest of moments what it might be to lift a knife and to drive the blade deep into their own flesh. For the sake of a bird.

The Storyteller concludes the story briskly. 'King Sivi cut from his own living flesh a piece of meat the size of a dove and tossed it to the hawk. The hawk swooped down hungrily to devour the warm meat. In the moment before he passed out, never to revive, the King smiled to see the dove fly free from his embrace and ascend up into the skies where, in a moment or two, she was gone from view.'

The storyteller slumps, exhausted from the telling. He wipes his forehead with the back of his hand. The sun has begun to disappear now, and the breezes are stronger. He realises that he is thirsty and he hopes that one of these people listening might offer him some water, or perhaps even some tea. He picks up his drum.

Bdoumm! Bdoumm! Bdoumm! BDOUMM!

There is silence in the audience. Little by little, the crowd filters away. Soon the Storyteller is left alone, and a thin moon shows itself in the darkening sky over the rooftops of the village. Nobody comes to offer him water, let alone tea. Never mind, he says to himself. He can drink to slake his thirst by the river. And tomorrow? He examines the skin of the drum thoughtfully. Tomorrow he will tell another story.

The villagers trail back to their homes, dissatisfied and ill at ease. Those who have television sets and satellite dishes turn them on in the hope that the flickering of images in front of them might serve to drive out their restlessness. Sitting there in the wavering dark, they find it impossible to get comfortable, as if something is pricking at them. They curse the Storyteller. They had not wanted a story about a king who cuts the flesh from his thigh for the sake of a mere bird. They had wanted an epic of great heroism and many battles. They had wanted love found and lost and found again. They had wanted a heroine abducted on the back of a horse (or a camel, or a jeep, or a helicopter, or an elephant—the precise means did not matter as much as the fact of abduction itself) by a villain with a paunch and a luxuriant moustache to twiddle. They had wanted the entrance of a dashing hero who could pluck the heroine from the jaws of death. The old man, they complain to each other as they flick through the channels, is out of touch. They curse themselves for even bothering to struggle out of their houses to hear his absurd tale. And they console themselves with the irritable thought: 'But it was only a story.'

And yet, that night, as they toss and turn in their beds, from time to time they reach down to touch their thighs, as if in the memory of a sharp pain that they had felt there long ago. In another lifetime, perhaps.

Neither Literalism nor Allegory

How is this story to be read? It seems that we can take it one of two ways. Firstly, we can either assume that this is reportage, that it tells of an event that actually happened, at some place and some time. This may, of course, stretch our credulity. We know that in the world which we inhabit doves and hawks do not talk. We know that neither in the present day nor in living memory have kings been so constituted that they make sacrifices with such ease. Nevertheless, as we shall see, these hurdles are not insurmountable, and it is possible (many people do) to put such objections to one side. On the other hand, we could go without our hunch that kings are not generally self-sacrificing and that birds do not generally speak in human language, and read the story allegorically. Of course doves and hawks do not talk, of course kings do not make such sacrifices, of course nobody would cut the flesh from their thigh in such a cavalier fashion, so therefore the story must be interpreted.[13]

The first of these readings, taking the story at face value, is one that, although it may seem odd, is not unusual in the Indian traditions. In this reading, the king is no ordinary petty monarch, but a *bodhisattva*, one who has set his heart upon liberation for all beings and who will be reborn again and again out of compassion for the liberation and welfare of all until he himself, purified by his compassionate deeds, attains his own liberation. To be sure, no ordinary king would act in such a way, this argument goes; but there are extraordinary beings in the world, and occasionally—implausible as this may seem—they even manifest as kings, prime ministers and the like. Even the talking animals are not an impediment to a literal translation.

The king, after all, is special. He has a deeper wisdom and insight than the rest of us. It is perhaps not that the animals say anything different from their usual speaking, it is just that the king is unusually attuned to what they are saying.[14] For such a reading to be possible we must assent to a chain of hypothetical reasoning: *if* we are to live innumerable lifetimes on end; *if* this interminability occasions in us a kind of claustrophobia; *if* acts of great compassion such as this may speed our liberation from this predicament; and *if* this cycle of rebirth is indeed a predicament, something from which it might be worth attempting to make our escape, *then* the story no longer seems unreasonable. Our thighs are fat, and there are many thin hawks—or dogs, or cats, or neighbours—who could benefit from some more meat; and if only we have the wisdom to recognise the fact, we too will benefit, for our liberation will be hastened and the sum total of our sufferings will, at the end of the day, be lesser. Precisely such a literal interpretation seems to be suggested in the *Siksa Samuccaya* where the Buddha addresses Maitreya, asking, 'What thinkest thou, Ajita Was the king of Kashi foolish, who gave his flesh to the hawk to save the dove?', in answer to which Maitreya says, 'He was not, my Lord' (Bendall and Rouse 2000, 99).

The curious thing about all this, however, is that when placed in the context of traditional Indian Buddhist beliefs about rebirth and liberation, on this reading, the king could equally be said to be acting from rational self-interest and to be acting from compassion. It is made clear in innumerable texts that the path to Buddhahood—that is, to full liberation from all suffering—involves the practice of just these kinds of self-sacrificing actions through innumerable lifetimes. It is a long, hard slog, but each time I cut out my thigh and die in agony, I am reborn in a new body, a little closer to my goal. Thus we could extract from the story an ethical maxim for aspirant Buddhas: *it is good to sever our limbs and use them as food when confronted by hungry animals*. Unconvinced? Well, the argument might say, that's your problem. You simply aren't cut out (or at least not yet) for Buddhahood.

Few, I suspect, would find it easy to subscribe to this as an ethical maxim; but what is of interest here is not the question of whether or not we can subscribe to this maxim at all, but instead the question of what happens to the shudder that runs through the story when we undertake such a reading. For somehow, in the act of interpretation, the story has been stripped of its power to trouble us. The king's act of compassion, looked at in this context, is reduced to an act of calculus. Any rational agent—indeed, as the economists say, any self-interested rational agent—possessed of the same knowledge and understanding as the king, would act in such a way that their interests might be best served. The only problem with this is that in the many tellings and retellings of the story, it simply does not seem to happen that the king has to ponder his act, that he has to engage in some form of Utilitarian hedonic calculus before he takes the knife and cuts into his flesh. His action is simply a response to the suffering that is before him. So we must consider the other, apparently more attractive, possibility. If a literal reading seems both to strip the story of its power, and also to lead to unacceptable ethical consequences, perhaps it might be more appropriate to read the story as allegory. We could, for example, claim that the story speaks of the burdens of power: it tells how a king, or any ruler, must himself be torn apart by the conflicting demands of his subjects. We could say that the story speaks of how we should be considerate towards our fellow creatures. But once again in this allegorical or symbolic reading, the story itself is subtly nudged out of the way by the propositions that replace it. When we reduce the story down to the proposition *sometimes it's hard to be a king* or to the imperative *be nice to animals*, unquestionably something is lost. Imperatives and propositions such as these completely fail to do justice to the story. When we are left with such bland maxims, it is clear that we have failed to give the story its due.[15]

If the story of King Sivi shares anything with that of Abraham and Isaac it is, at the very least, that it horrifies us with the sheer scandal of its central act, a scandal that seems to stand in the way of our capacity for interpretation, to resist our attempts to reduce the story to ethical propositions or maxims. It is not easy to see precisely how this story could act as a propaedeutic to ethics in Ricoeur's sense, nor what possibilities the story could usefully feed back into our own lives.

There is, however, a third course. Annabella Pitkin notes that such accounts of responses to suffering as are found in the Buddhist traditions take their power from the very fact that they are scandalous. Pitkin claims that such scandalous approaches to ethics 'cut away complacency and force us to confront a contradiction to the self-absorbed self', while not permitting us to 'slip away from the confrontation with what is hardest' (Pitkin 2001, 245); and in this, she notes, they bear some relationship to the ethical excess that is encountered in Levinas. Whether this is so or not, it is clear that in losing our interpretations of the story—either through allegorising it or through reading the story literally—we have lost both the story and the shudder that runs through it. Instead, we are left with an ethical maxim that is either so bland as to be worthless or so extreme that we simply cannot accept it. However, we should also remember the framing story of the villagers, their fleshly shuddering, their insomnia, the remembered pain of an event that never happened.[16] There is something in this shudder that is troubling, that we cannot easily overcome.

It might, of course, be tempting to dismiss the story as a 'bad story.' It doesn't seem to teach us anything explicit. It doesn't tell us what to do or how to live. It makes us restless and uncomfortable. Nonetheless, the judgement that the story is a 'bad' story and that stories are only useful that provide workable and stable maxims that have an instrumental value in how we go about our lives, is unjustified; and it is hard not to suspect that such dismissals are merely a way of evading the discomfort of the shudder that stories such as this occasion in us. Stories may turn out to have a value that goes beyond their ability to provide us with clear, unambiguous maxims, as Benjamin hinted at when he pointed out that the explicit peddling of moral maxims is the final state of decline of a story: 'A proverb, one might say, is a ruin which stands on the site of an old story and in which a moral twines about a gesture like ivy around a wall' (Benjamin 2006, 162). Perhaps it is necessary to move in the reverse direction, from the ivy to the ruined walls, to rebuild our understanding of the spaces that together make up the stories that we construct.

Turbulent Crossings

Scandalous tales such as that of Abraham and Isaac or the Jataka of King Sivi, by virtue of the sheer difficulty of deriving workable ethical maxims from them, force us to reconsider whether an interpretative approach can provide us with the last word in thinking through what stories are and what they do. As Kierkegaard says, such an approach simply falls short in giving a story its due. And yet these seem also to be stories that carry with them a certain kind of ethical force, if we could only work out how. So we need another approach, one that does not seek to resolve stories into propositional understandings, one that pays attention to the embodied nature of our experience and that does not miss the shudder of thought. At this point, then, perhaps a few naïve phenomenological questions are in order. Let us return for a moment to the beginning of the story of Kikori and Fly:

It is winter. Outside sleet is spattering against the window. I am sitting in the armchair, and I am tired. Tired and ill-tempered.

You look at me. 'Tell me a story,' you say.

I do not want to tell you a story. 'I am too tired,' I say.

'Tell me a story,' you repeat.

I try to tell you that a story requires effort, that I have had a hard day... But as I am explaining all this, I realise that you are not going to give up, and that it would be easier, all things considered, to get on with it and tell a story. 'What story do you want to hear?' I sigh.

You smile. 'Tell me about Kikori and Fly,' you suggest.

And so I do.

Kikori and Fly live, I tell you, in a cave. It is dark and unpleasant; and one day Kikori, tired of these conditions, has a thought: 'I will invent a house!' he says.

'What's a house?' asks Fly.

'I don't know,' Kikori confesses, 'I've not invented it yet.'

If we want to be attentive to ethics as *experience*, then we need to attend much more carefully to the texture of experience itself. It was Kant who wrote that time and space were conditions of the possibility of any experience whatever. That is to say, there is no experience that is not bound up, in some way or another, with time or with space. And yet reflecting on the curious experience of storytelling begins to suggest that the texture of the times and the spaces of experience is rather more complex than we might at first suspect.

Let us begin with what seems like a naïve phenomenological question: *where does a story take place*? With regard to the story of Kikori and Fly, the answer to this question at first appears to be relatively simple. It takes place in a cave in the forest. 'Which cave?' we might then ask, to which the irritable answer might be, 'Does it matter?' 'Which jungle?' 'Who cares?'

Perhaps we cannot locate a single place out there in the world where the story happens. But if this is so, then we should ask another question: when you confront this story, which cave do you, as a reader, imagine? I noted above, that as a philosopher, I could not help but think of Plato, regardless of how apposite such a thought may or may not have been (and the suspicion must be that it is not particularly apposite) to the original context of the story; but what is the cave that *you* think of when I tell you a story that takes place in a cave? Is it made of caves that you have known and dreamed of in the past? How is it constituted? Is it a pre-existing cave that you draw up whenever I say the word 'cave', or does it emerge in the telling of this particular story? If I told the story a second time, would it take place in the same cave?

And why stop here? It is possible to muster further naïve questions about the spaces of this particular story, for the story of Kikori and Fly (like the story of the man who reads the story of Abraham and Isaac, like the story of King Sivi and the dove) is framed in another story, the story of the telling, in winter, with sleet on the window. The story has at least two locations, it takes place in two worlds not one: there is a cave in a jungle, and there is a place where the storyteller is telling the tale. Are these two worlds in the frame of the story nested like Russian dolls, or is their relationship more complex than this? Perhaps we need to look further still, exploring still other frames. There is also the place where you, the reader, are reading about the jungle and the winter, where you are reading about the rain that falls in the jungle, and the sleet that splatters the window. Perhaps you are sitting at a bus stop in the sleet. Perhaps you are in the jungle. Perhaps you are seated at a desk. How do I know? But wherever you are, this makes a difference as well, if it is indeed the case that we do not approach the story as disembodied readers. For every story that we encounter, we encounter it somewhere, as the novelist Calvino recognised when he offered the following advice to his readers:

> Find the most comfortable position: seated, stretched out, curled up, or lying flat. Flat on your back, on your side, on your stomach. In an easy chair, on the sofa, in the rocker, the deck chair, on the hassock. In the hammock, if you have a hammock. On top of your bed, of course, or in the bed. You can even stand on your hands, head down, in the yoga position. With the book upside down, naturally. (Calvino 2007, 3)

The question of where the story takes place does not lead us to a neat Cartesian grid-point where we can stick a pin: experiential space is simply not mapped like this. Instead, the more we dwell upon the question, the more we realise that in the telling of a story, our sense of space itself becomes something fluid and complex. The story is, in a very real sense, neither here nor there. It opens up its own locales, but these locales are temporary, shifting, and curiously hard to locate with any precision. And this is not just the case with stories (although stories may help remind us of this): it is the case with all experience whatsoever. We are here, and we are not here. We are sitting on the bus and dreaming of being at home; or we are at home and dreaming of how, had things been otherwise, we might be sitting on a bus and dreaming of a quite different home. And as we are dreaming on the bus, outside the window the signs and images flit past, and the mind takes them in even if we don't ever seem to notice, and behind us we realise, just now, there has been somebody talking to a friend about when they were in Paris, but we didn't catch what they were saying and now it is too late, and that itch on our knee still hasn't gone away...

Here, the multiple framing of the *Yogavasishtha*—far from

being a rhetorical extravagance—begins instead to look more like a way of bringing to our attention the overlapping complexity of any experience whatsoever.

So it may be that we need some new questions that can do justice to these complex, quivering, unstable locales. Not 'what is the space of the story?' but perhaps something like, 'how do experiences of space emerge in the telling of a story?' Neither entirely the world of the reader (or the teller, or the listener) nor the world of the text, we find the opening up of spaces that, by virtue of being both multiple and fluctuating, cannot be mapped in a Cartesian fashion, but that nevertheless are traversed in the telling, so each telling is a crossing of multiple thresholds. And in this complexity, as Serres writes, 'the body knows that it has crossed to the outside, that it has just entered another world. Space and our stories are full of such thresholds: the axis of the river, the arm of the sea, through which one swims' (Serres 1997, 10). Why the body? Because, however unmappable by the mind these many spaces of the story may be, we tellers and listeners—our minds processing myriad fluctuating streams of information that pour in through our senses —are nevertheless single. We are one flesh. And this fleshy organism is capable of holding more than a single thought; it quivers with unresolved contradictions and tensions; it hums with life. We enter into a story, and all seems in order; but at some point—who can say when?—we find we are out of our depth, we have lost all reference, and the mind can no longer keep hold of the threads that are unfolding. The body takes over as the currents of the story carry us onwards, even though we can make no sense of the acts of King Sivi or Abraham, even if we do not know whether 'Fly' refers to a creature with fly nature or with human nature or with both, even if we forget to ask how it can be that a woodpecker, or a hawk or a dove, can talk.

This sense of the multiple thresholds and spaces that open

up in the telling of the story gives us a way of thinking through Kierkegaard's shudder of thought, but without retreating to some idea of inner truth. The spaces that open in the telling of a tale are not single. They are neither the world of the reader, nor the world of the text, nor some precisely defined third that might function as a hybrid of the two, but instead, as we listen to the tale, as we swim the channel of the story, either confidently or on the brink of drowning, we find ourselves,

> inhabiting both banks and haunting the middle where the two directions converge, as well as the direction of the flowing river, and that of the wind, of the uneasy list of the swim, of the numerous intentions that produce decisions; in this river within the river... Do you believe it to be triple? You are still mistaken, it is multiple. (Serres 1997, 6-7)

This, surely, is a form of phenomenology, even if it doesn't at first glance look much like it. Phenomenology since Husserl has always operated by a form of 'reduction', by the bracketing out of assumptions in its quest to rigorously describe experience. But perhaps philosophy will not succeed in such description until it starts to look rather less like philosophy, until it realises that what looks like philosophy is a blunt tool when it comes to describing with sufficient care the liquid tapestry of experience. It can be useful, at times, to bracket out the trappings of philosophy themselves, and to ask what other resources we may have at our disposal.[17]

Let us return, then, to the things themselves. Listen to your breath as you hear a story. Observe how, when the king plunges the knife, the air enters your body sharply. Pay attention to how you sigh as the two lovers at last meet. Notice how your body responds and cannot but respond. Notice also how—as you grasp for a thought, a concept, a word, an idea—your eyes gaze off into the middle distance as if you are looking for the words somewhere in space. Feel the back arch and unarch, the fingers flex and unflex, the toes curl and uncurl, with the rhythms of the telling. Where does the story take place? If we must commit ourselves to saying that it takes place anywhere, to finding a centre of gravity of this mixed locale, then let us place this centre in the body and not in the mind. This body, made of stuff that we share with the world, porous and leaky, capable of trembling and shuddering, made up of endless overlappings, of shifting, multiple layerings, is neither an idealised subject over which I can claim utter sovereignty nor a cold object towards which I can be indifferent. Here in this body, I feel the conflicting pull of Kikori and Fly's rainforest and the sleet upon the windowsill; it is here in this very body that I feel what it is to open your eyes in surprise as a dove falls from the sky into your lap. It is here that I shudder, because I have a body.

Amid all the hubbub, within this quivering frame of flesh that shudders before suffering and the thought of suffering, there may be enough room to open up spaces—to open up many spaces, even—for those things that make life worth living: kindness, for example, or attentiveness, or knowledge.

And yet, thinking back to that afternoon in Darjeeling, it was not just that we were jostled by the crowd in the market-place, that the market was crowded, that we felt ourselves to be lacking in sufficient space to respond to the suffering man's need: it was also that we told ourselves that we simply did not have the time to respond. Time, then, is the subject of the next chapter.

7

STORIES ABOUT TIME

A storyteller once told me that in Romania they begin their tales in the following way: *It was a time, and it was no time...* The precision of this is impressive. Storytelling is—as Rosenzweig knew—a way of thinking that is attentive to the experience of time, down to the finest detail: thus 'it was *a* time'. And yet, at the same time, the times of stories, just like the spaces of stories, seem hard to pinpoint exactly in this or that time: hence 'it was *no* time'.

But when we are talking about time, we must also talk about space, because in the frame of a story, as in experience in general, it seems impossible to thoroughly draw apart the threads of time and of space (Assad 1999, 95). They are bound up with each other beyond any disentangling (Turner 1998, 119-22). The Russian literary theorist Bakhtin refers to this entanglement as *chronotope*:

> We will give the name chronotope (literally, 'time-space') to the intrinsic connectedness of temporal and spatial relationships that are artistically expressed in literature... In the literary artistic chronotope, spatial and temporal

indicators are fused into one carefully thought-out, concrete whole. Time, as it were, thickens, takes on flesh, becomes artistically visible; likewise, space becomes charged and responsive to the movements of time, plot and history. This intersection of axes and fusion of indicators characterises the artistic chronotope. (Bakhtin 1982, 84)

Here one might wonder whether Bakhtin goes far enough. Certainly, there is such an entanglement of time and space within literature, but this entanglement is not only limited to literary artistic creations which are well thought-out wholes. It might be more accurate to say that *all* experience—not merely experience composed into a literary whole by a writer of skill and artfulness—has a chronotopic form. We never experience pure, atemporal spaces; and we never experience pure time severed from space. However carefully we may divide the two for the purposes of analysis, in experience they come lumped together. Experience is temporal and spatial, both at the same time. Not only this, but this experience of time and space is never neutral, but is always laden with curiously intangible properties, with a particular mood or feel, associated with webs of memories, images, ideas and stories. Call to mind any strong memory, and notice how it is possible to trace these strange, shimmering threads that give that memory its precision. As Ramanujan has pointed out in one of his studies of Indian systems of thought, despite Kant's claims that space and time are merely conditions of the possibility of experience, 'even space and time... [are] not uniform and neutral, but have properties, varying specific densities, that affect those who dwell in them' (Ramanujan 1998, 45).[1] Once we see that our experiences of spaces and times are neither uniform nor neutral, we find ourselves returning to the rich conception of experience that is proposed by Benjamin—that mixed, interwoven and multi-layered tapestry in liquid motion.

In his book *Time and Narrative*, Ricoeur suggests that while all stories are stories of time—which is to say that they take time in the telling, that their unfolding is a matter *of* time—only a few are stories *about* time, that is, in only a few stories is it the 'very experience of time that is at stake' (Ricoeur 1990, 101). It seems that here Ricoeur is being unnecessarily restrictive in his idea of what it might mean to say that a story is about time. If we accept that, on the one hand, time and space are themselves impossible to fully disentangle, and on the other hand that these times and spaces always have properties and are never neutral; and if we further pay attention to the fact that the times of the story unfold in the telling, a telling which brings together a whole range of shifting, complex times and spaces, then we must conclude that time is at stake not only in all stories, but ultimately in all experience whatsoever. The question is not that of discovering in which particular stories time is at stake, but rather that of asking *how* precisely, in any story whatsoever, time is at stake.

To explore this, let us turn to a story taken from the *Yogavasishtha*. Once again, it is the story of a king—this time one called Lavana—who meets with a certain magician. We do not know precisely when, in the distant past, the story is set. Let us say, then, that it was a time, and it was no time. And although the original story concerns a magician, we might take a few liberties and—mindful of Levinas's warning that stories themselves are a form of sorcery—imagine that the particular magic that this sorcerer weaves is the magic of telling a damned good tale. This is admittedly a small departure from the letter or the text, but it is certainly not a departure from the spirit, as in the tradition from which the *Yogavasishtha* comes, both stories and magic are seen as things that can lead us to a deeper appreciation of the endless play of *maya* or of illusion that some Indian metaphysicians tell us is the ultimate nature of the things

(O'Flaherty 1986, 114-22). So, almost inevitably, we are once again concerned with a story about the telling of a story.

Travels in Time and Space

King Lavana was bored. Sitting on his throne, the days passed slowly. His courtiers came to him and said, 'Your Highness, a magician is here to see you.'

The king sighed. 'Send him in.'

The magician entered, a ragged man with bits of food caught in his beard. 'I warn you now,' said Lavana, 'if you do that rope trick again, you will be beheaded.'

'Of course, your majesty, that is indeed a cheap trick,' the magician conceded.[2]

'And if you turn a block of wood into an elephant, I will be similarly unimpressed.'[3]

The magician inclined his head. 'As would any man of wisdom.'

'What, then, is your magic? Where is your bag of tricks?'

'I have no bag of tricks. I have only these.' The magician pointed towards his own eyes. The king met his gaze. Then the magician started to speak.

All at once, everything changed. The Prime Minister, the servants, the magician himself, the throne room—it was as if all these dissolved away, and the king found himself in a field before a wild horse. Impressed by the nobility of the steed, the king decided he would ride it.

He began to pursue the horse, but it remained always just out of reach, leading him across fields and through forests into distant territories. At last, the king, exasperated, lunged at the steed, caught hold of its mane and pulled himself up on the animal's back. The horse reared and leapt into the air. They fell upwards, tumbling through the clouds as they hurtled over the trees, valleys, meadows. Soon, the king felt his grip begin to slip away. He fell, landing in the cross-arms of a tree. A family of monkeys gawped at him. The horse was gone.

The king clambered down to the ground. He was entirely lost. He started to walk.

Lavana walked for days, living on fruit, sleeping on the forest floor. Eventually, when all his energy had gone, he collapsed and lay as if dead. A Candala woman with a hare-lip came and woke him. 'Who are you?' the king asked.

'It does not matter.'

'I am hungry. What is in your basket?'

'Food for my father.'

'Give it to me.'

'Why should I? Who are you?'

'I am a king.' The king sounded less than certain.

'In that case, I cannot feed you for it is not proper to my caste. I am an untouchable, and you are of the warrior caste.'

The king winced. 'Then I am not a king,' he said. 'Please, give me some food.'

The woman thought. 'I will give you food if you agree to marry me.'

The king knew he had no choice. 'Then I will marry you,' he said.

They were married the following day, and they lived together in a hut roofed with coconut thatch. Lavana became a huntsman, spearing game in the forest. His wife became pregnant and in due course bore him four sons. Lavana wore clothes of bark, and his hair became matted.

Several years later, famine and drought struck the land. The waters in the pools dried up. The animals fled for places where food was more abundant or else they died of hunger. The trees stood naked on the scorched plains, and the crops failed. Lavana and his family left home, walking through the stricken land in search of food. His three eldest sons soon turned against him, saying that he was an old fool, incapable of caring for them. They left in search of their own destinies.

Now there only remained Lavana, his youngest son, and his wife, who was becoming increasingly thin, bitter and ill-tempered. The three of them kept on walking. Then, one day, by an enormous rock that stood in the middle of a plain, the youngest son collapsed and could move no more.

Lavana spoke to his wife and son. 'Do not worry. I will find food for you. Just stay where you are. I will find meat. I'll go and light the fire now, behind the rock over there. I will call you when the meat is on the fire. Then you must wait a while before coming to join the feast. Bring a little salt if you have any.'

The wife and son did as he asked. They heard the fire begin to crackle behind the rock. Lavana called out, 'Do not move! Come when the fire has died down! I am preparing the meat. Do not take it out of the fire until it is well-cooked.'

Then Lavana jumped into the fire.

The moment the flames touched his skin, Lavana felt the world slip away from beneath him. He blacked out momentarily; and when he came round, his hands were clutching the arms of the throne. His Prime Minister was leaning forwards with an anxious look on his face.

'Where is he?' the king demanded. 'Bring the magician to me! That was quite some trick! I want to reward him!'

'The storyteller, your majesty?' the Prime Minister asked. 'He left just a moment ago.'

King Lavana lives a lifetime in a few moments through the power of the storyteller-magician. But which is more fundamental: the lifetime, or the few moments? In his own retelling of the myth, the nineteenth century Telugu poet Guru Jada Appa Rao has the king marvelling at this strange blurring of times, asking, 'Have seven minutes lasted seven years? Or have seven years been captured in seven minutes?' (O'Flaherty 1986, 169). The time that King Lavana lives while under the magician's spell cannot be clearly mapped onto the time that he lives when sitting spellbound on the throne. The two times are clearly not the same—Lavana lives years under the spell while the magician stays for a few moments (or for seven minutes) in the throne room; but neither are they absolutely different from each other, for Lavana-as-Candala never ceases also to be Lavana-as-king, even when he himself has forgotten his kingship. Here, we are not being asked to think philosophically about the complex nature of time, but instead, we are asked to witness it in action, as the story unfolds. There is no single clear answer to the question, 'How long does the magician's spell last?' Both a lifetime and a few moments.

The times within the frame of the story, however, are not the only times at stake; for, as with the spaces of the story discussed above, we must also take into account the times of the telling, my time and your time. Of these times, none is fundamental, no one of them is somehow a base point onto which we can map all the others. Because of the impossibility of compressing the story into a neat philosophical framework, Doniger, writing of the relationship between *Yogavasishtha* and the philosophical traditions of India, notes that often stories such as these go further than philosophy, that 'the story was always bigger, more profound, than any explicit argument that could be made to gloss it... The story is a river whose fish keep jumping out' (O'Flaherty 1990, 131).[4] It is not a matter of reducing the story to a set of philosophical propositions. Instead, it is a matter of taking seriously the complex experience of time to which the story attests. And while it might be tempting to reduce this complexity by taking one of the times at play in the story as the 'base' time onto which we could map all the other times of the story, this decision would be one that ignored the fact of mixture, the fact that the times and spaces within the telling are not merely parallel strands that can be disentangled, but are mixed beyond any separation. One can no more extract from the whole the various times that are mixed together in making a story than one can extract eggs, flour and sugar from a fully-baked cake.

If there are no pure, unmixed times and unmixed spaces, then neither can there be any such thing as pure, unmixed subjects or selves. As selves, we are tangled up in the many times, spaces and rhythms of the world. We are not separate. We are bound to a degree, but not absolutely, things of shifting borders, knots amid the countless knottings-together of the world. And in all of this knotting and unknotting and constant shifting, time appears to us not as an abstraction—whether conceived as a continuous line that we can divide up infinitesi-mally, or as a series of discrete instants—but as a mixture of many different currents and rhythms. There is no reason to limit the idea of mixtures of times and spaces only to the special case of storytelling. Instead, stories such as that of Lavana merely bring to our attention some of the characteristics of experience in general, characteristics that—perhaps on account of our philosophical commitments—we may have overlooked. Serres writes,

> The customary, I hardly dare call it ordinary or basic, experience of time is that it, at times, is composed of instants, and that, at times, it flows by, devoid of units. It is discontinuous and it is continuous. It passes and it does not pass. It comes back on itself, sometimes, and sometimes, it lapses or is lost, absented. More than present, through this redundancy, and more than vanished, in its lability. Time becomes expansive and contracts, all at once dense and soon spread out... Time is lacunary and sporadic, it is a badly

stitched tatter, it passes, loose, a mosaic. Time is pure multiplicity. (Serres 1995, 115)[5]

Pure multiplicity: that is to say, there is nowhere in time (and nowhere in space, and nowhere in those things we identify as subjects, and nowhere in those things to which we give the name 'objects') that escapes this mixture. There are no absolutely self-enclosed entities to be found, anywhere. We are imprecise in our boundaries, permeable, continually shifting, semi-stable.

But perhaps to understand this lacunary, sporadic experience of time, we would do well to put theory again to one side, and to return once again to the telling of stories.

Kant meets Atuf: The Birth of Time

If time is a badly stitched tatter, then questions in which philosophers have long delighted concerning the nature of time seem curiously beside the point. Questions such as that of the origin of time, even questions about the nature of time, assume a kind of orderliness and unity to time that both our stories and our experience call into question.[6] It is for this reason that it has already been necessary to move from talking about the origin of time to the origins of *times*, from discussing the nature of *time* to discussing the natures of times. This is a distinction that the following story from the Tanimbar Islands in Maluku, Indonesia makes clear.[7]

It was before the beginning of time that Atuf came to the Tanimbar islands. A nobleman from the island of Babar, he was overthrown by his slaves and fled into exile. Taking a war canoe, he set sail for Tanimbar with his sisters Inkelu, Yaum

Aratwenan and Mangmwatabun. They came ashore at the village of Sifnana and looked around at the sorry place that was now their home.

At that time, there were no rivers in Tanimbar, and the land was jumbled up with the sea. The moon and stars slept within the belly of the sun which, heavy and immobile, hung low on the horizon. There was neither night nor day, for the night and day are measured by the sun's course across the skies and the turning of the stars on their slow axis at night. There was no waxing or waning of the moon, neither were there changing seasons. All was dark and cold and stagnant. The people back then were strange, too: not quite human. They lived out in the forest. Some wore tails, others had many arms or heads, positioned in strange places. They did not eat cooked food, for there was no fire. It was no place for a nobleman. So Atuf took a spear—a spear that some claim was once in the possession of Ubila'a, the supreme deity, himself—and began to slice the earth from the sea, hacking the smaller islands off the bulk of Yamdena, carving out a new world. When his work on Yamdena was finished, he equipped his war canoe, and took some slaves, ready to sail to the eastern horizon. Before he left, he and his sister Inkelu danced together on the bows of the boat like noble frigate birds, the slow, stooping dance that is still danced in Tanimbar down to the present day. It was the last time they were to see each other. Atuf cast off from the shore.

Stowed in the bottom of the canoe were clam shells filled with coconut milk, and as the party sailed to the sun and the heat became more intense, they bathed their bodies in the cooling milk to protect them from the burning rays. The closer they came to the horizon, the lower the sky hung over their heads. They sliced off the top of the mast to avoid becoming stuck between the sky and the sea. The sun was close now. The sea boiled angrily about them, and the boards of the canoe began to smoke and blacken. Raising a wooden plank to shelter him from the savage fire of the sun, Atuf stood, took aim, and thrust the spear into the heart of the furnace. The sun shattered into a million parts. A large piece plummeted into the sea with a hiss and a plume of steam. When it rose again, it had become cool and white, and became known as the moon. Countless tiny fragments were scattered across the sky, and these became the stars. Dripping the red blood of dawn, the sun rose and cast light over Tanimbar for the first time.

Atuf met a tragic end. He was never to set foot in the village of Sifnana again, nor was he to long enjoy the fruits of his heroism. As the victorious party sailed back home, they stopped off on the cape of Lamdesar in the northern part of the archipelago where the mango trees grow upside down, putting their roots up into the air and their branches into the soil, dropping their fruits upward into the sky. Atuf went ashore, asking his slaves to wait while he relieved himself. He squatted down to go about his business and, as he emptied his bowels, he stuck fast to the ground. Atuf had turned to stone. He remains there to this day, even if the mango trees have long gone, fixed in stone on the cape of Lamdesar, shitting.

Atuf's slaves returned home without him, but when they stepped ashore, they turned into tree shrews and possums, scuttled into the forest and were gone.[8]

What is striking about this Tanimbarese tale is that, although it is a story about the birth of time, this birth of time is seen as a purely local affair. The Tanimbarese story has no interest in the origins of time in an absolute cosmological sense. The story accounts for the origins of both the time and the space of the Tanimbar islands, for the local appearance of the sun as it rises daily from the sea, for the shape of the islands, the capes, the rivers. Everybody knows that before Atuf's action the sun of

Babar was not the same as the sun of Tanimbar. In Babar—Atuf's home before he was driven out by his slaves—the sun travelled in its course across the sky and the moon waxed and waned. Then he arrived in Tanimbar and found that there the sun squatted low on the horizon, dark and oppressive. It seems that we have two suns, one for each locality. However, at the same time, everybody also knows that, although on his arrival the sun of Tanimbar was not the sun of Babar, once Atuf had performed his heroic deed, the sun of Babar was now no different from the sun of Tanimbar and between the two archipelagos there was only one sun.

This, then, is not a 'creation myth', that category under which many stories of beginnings are subsumed, if by 'creation myth' we mean an account of the coming-to-be of the world or the universe as a whole, some kind of ultimate origin of things in general. The idea of totality suggested by the term 'creation myth' simply does not apply here. But, if this is not a creation myth, we might ask, then what is it? I would suggest that, in part, it is a pretty neat solution to the first of Kant's antinomies of pure reason, in which an old philosophical chestnut is dispatched with a minimum of fuss and with nothing in the way of technical jargon, but in a fashion that, perhaps surprisingly for the philosophers, is not that distant from Kant's own. This is how Kant frames the problem:

> Thesis: the world has a beginning in time, and in space it is also enclosed in boundaries... Antithesis: the world has no beginning and no bounds in space, but is infinite with regard to both time and space. (Kant 1999, 471)

I myself had a problem with this antinomy long before I had heard of Kant. As a somewhat metaphysically-inclined child, I used to lie in bed and imagine the limits of time or of space. And whenever I imagined a limit, I imagined adding another second (if what I was thinking about was time), or another inch (if what I was thinking about was space). Because it seemed I could easily do so, it also seemed that there could be no limits. But then I tried to imagine unlimited time and space, and that too seemed to present me with all manner of difficulties. The same difficulty occurs with stories. In his book on Greek myth, Roberto Calasso repeatedly asks the question, 'But where did it all begin?' (Calasso 1994), a question that leads him on a wild goose chase in pursuit of a point that is always out of reach. If we set a beginning point, this beginning seems arbitrary: why begin precisely here and not before? What caused the first cause? Who moved the self-moved mover? Nobody, the theologians reply, because the self-moved mover, by definition, needs nothing except itself to move itself. Then what of the universe as a whole? reply the sceptics. Why not just call everything that exists, as a totality, a self-moved mover? And so the debate goes on, seemingly without hope of resolution. Kant points out that this irresolvable antinomy arises because of a more fundamental error, the error of seeing the world in terms of a totality at all. Thus he writes:

Accordingly, the antinomy of pure reason in its cosmological ideas is removed by showing that it is merely dialectical and a conflict due to an illusion arising from the fact that one has applied the idea of absolute totality, which is valid only as a condition of things in themselves, to appearances that exist only in representation, and that, if they constitute a series, exist in the successive regress but otherwise do not exist at all. If the world is a whole existing in itself, then it is either finite or infinite. Now the first as well as the second alternative is false (according to the proof offered above for the antithesis on the one side and the thesis on the other). Thus it is also false that the world (the sum of all appearances) is a whole existing in itself. (Kant 1999, 519)

Kant's resolution of the problem is this: if time and space are conditions of the possibility of the appearance of any phenomena whatsoever, but not properties of things in themselves, then we are making an error talking about the world—which is nothing other than the sum of all appearances—as a thing in itself. Not only this, but if the world is not a thing in itself, then it makes no sense to ask about its finitude or infinity.

The Tanimbarese escape from the antinomy takes a different route but works by virtue of the same refusal: the refusal to see the world as a totality of synthesisable times. However, rather than going in the direction of making time a transcendental condition for things, they take the alternative route of seeing time as a purely local phenomenon. The time of Babar is not the time of Tanimbar.[9]

Kant, in the long run, does not renounce the idea of totality itself, only the claim that we can know it; he does not renounce the idea of that which is transcendental, only the possibility of its attainment. The Tanimbarese, on the other hand, in their stories and their myths do not demand global totalities. Instead, they are concerned with localities each of which may have its own times and its own spaces. If the story of Atuf is about the genesis of a local time, it is also a story that is rooted in local spaces. If you go to the Tanimbar islands and are fortunate enough to be shown around by somebody old enough to remember the stories, they will tell you: that is the cape where Atuf shat for the final time; this is the place where he landed, by the bay at Sifnana; and (pointing to the horizon) there is the beach—over in the Kai islands—where the spear spilt the blood of the sun. Go and look if you like. You can still see that the sand is red!

This local knowledge—always shifting, and subject to change—is a very different thing from the kind of absolutely foundational science of which Husserl dreamed. It is different also from the kind of everyday, empirical piecing-together of knowledge that makes up a lot of what we call 'science'. But as my Tanimbarese friends knew all too well, there are other kinds of knowledge that must take their place alongside the knowledge of the sciences. 'You come here with your science and you tell us that you know what is true and what is not,' they used to tell me, 'but if I were to take you into the forest, what good would your science do you? How long would you survive? You and your science would die in a single night. Whereas we —we would live.' In this they were unquestionably right: if I were to cross Yamdena and I had to choose for a guide between the self-proclaimed scientist Husserl, with all his certainties and general principles and laws, and an illiterate Tanimbarese villager whose knowledge was local, I would go for the latter option, almost every time.

Gods, Stories and Origins

Stories that speak of the origin of things as a whole are, in one sense, Aristotelian, in that they attempt to trace everything back to a first cause. Yet we would do well to remind ourselves of Calasso's caution that we can never find a pure beginning in the world, and that the self-enclosure of an Aristotelian story is not as complete as it might look.

There is, in fact, a curious parallel between Aristotle's account of stories, and Aristotle's account of gods. When he describes how a story begins with a beginning 'which is not itself necessarily after anything else' (1450b), he could equally well be describing an Aristotelian God. To follow necessarily, after all, is to be contingent upon something else. But something that does not follow necessarily from anything else has its own necessity. Aristotle writes in the *Metaphysics*:

> The first principle or primary being is not movable either in itself or accidentally, but produces the primary eternal and

single movement. But since that which is moved must be moved by something, and the first mover must be in itself unmovable, and eternal movement must be produced by something eternal and a single movement by a single thing, and since we see that besides the simple spatial movement of the universe, which we say the first and unmovable substance produces, there are other spatial movements—those of the planets—which are eternal (for a body which moves in a circle is eternal and unresting; we have proved these points in the physical treatises), each of these movements also must be caused by a substance both unmovable in itself and eternal. (1073a)

Aristotelian gods, like Aristotelian stories, exist self-subsistently in pure, unmixed times. In the same way that, in the *Poetics*, Aristotle suggests that a story creates its own time in which it is self-sufficient, so in the *Metaphysics* he suggests that a God is self-sufficient and complete within its time. The parallel is precise. But one has to wonder whether any story in the world—or, for that matter any god—ever measures up to the kind of austere vision that Aristotle proposes. Because if stories never live alone, the evidence seems to be that gods, by and large, are far from Aristotelian in their daily lives. They often hold conversations, so the experts tell us; they express wishes; sometimes, it appears, they even write best-sellers. And while questions about the gods, questions such as 'What do they eat? What do they drink? How do they dress? What are their houses like?' (Sissa & Detienne 2000, 19) may seem to be absurd in the Aristotelian framework, once again this appearance of absurdity is only local. Aristotle's god would make little sense to the traditional Tanimbarese. Does this God who only thinks, they might ask, never pause and take a drink of palm-wine? After all, palm-wine can be remarkably beneficial when it comes to thinking.

The fact of the matter is that this strange God who has become a self-reflexive being, 'impassive and unalterable', entirely removed from the hubbub of the world, but upon whom nevertheless the entire hubbub depends, is a localised concern. Most gods, through most of history, have simply not been like this. And most of us know that gods drink nectar, that they seduce nymphs and write books, that they go to bed when it gets dark and get up when the sun dawns, that they are born (and—yes—that sometimes, too, they die),[10] that they have their likes and dislikes, their petty disagreements, their tetchy smitings, their squabbles, their acts of generosity, their interests. We need not, then, be seduced into believing the claims of Aristotelian gods that they are the only gods, any more than we need to be seduced into believing that Aristotelian stories are the only stories. Gods and stories are a part of the hubbub of the world.

In Tanimbar at least, where the name given to the supreme deity was Ubila'a, we find a god who is as far from the Aristotelian ideal as could be imagined, a god who sneaks around and gets himself involved in the affairs of men, as the following story shows:

> Once, it is said, in the village of Sifnana, yams started to go missing from the plantations. A child was appointed to guard the crops, and there he saw an old man with a beard that grew down over his stomach. The old man crept into the garden at night, carrying a spear. The child took hold of the spear and tied the thief to it by his beard. Then he called for his family to come and kill the thief. The old man confessed to being Ubila'a, and he pleaded for his life. The people of Sifnana struck a hard bargain and only relented after the god gave them his spear. The spear was the one that was later used by Atuf to pierce the earth and open up channels for fresh water to flow.[11]

Ubila'a—like Ka, like Baal, like the Old Testament Yahweh before he went into retreat and rejected all company, or before the philosophers got their hands on him, like Zeus and Hera— is a social god. This is not the kind of god who generally interests philosophers; but it has to be said that the philosophers' god is a curious character indeed, hardly representative of gods in general (in the same way, perhaps, that the philosopher is often a curious character, hardly representative of people in general). While most gods are willing to roll their sleeves up and get involved in the world of which they are a part, the philosopher's God not only pretends that he is not of the world, but also makes the claim that he has created it.[12] Ordinarily in philosophy (when we are not making allowances for the fact that it is a god who is making such peculiar claims) this is considered to be one of the gravest of sins: that of solipsism, the delusion that one exists *solus ipse*.

If we reject this solipsism, if we return to the everyday experience that has been laid bare by the stories we have been considering—experience in which spaces, times and selves are never self-enclosed or folded in upon themselves—then we are free to recognise that our stories, our gods and our selves all find their own identities and meanings here in the world, alongside others. And so, having perhaps developed a richer sense of the complexity of our experience of everyday times and spaces, this is the next task: through the medium of stories, to begin to try and think about the nature of otherness, and about the ethics of the relations that we have with the many others—other peoples, other stories, other gods, other creatures—amongst whom we find ourselves.

8

STORIES ABOUT OTHERS

I t is a banal observation that we live in a world of otherness, a world of difference. I am different from you; we are different from them; sometimes, even, I claim that I am different from myself, protesting, 'I was not in my right mind,' or 'I don't know what got into me,' or, 'I'm not feeling myself today.' Difference, of course, is not limited only to selves. We know that the world outside is different from the world inside, up is different from down, left and right are not the same. Morning and evening, summer and winter, sickness and health, wealth and poverty... the list could go on for ever.

But which, amongst all of these kinds of difference, is the difference *that makes a difference*? For Levinas, the answer is clear: the true difference—the difference that truly makes a difference—is that between myself and another person. So, famously, he writes 'The absolutely other is the Other [person]' (Levinas 1969, 39).[1] In this relationship with the other person, Levinas insists there is a difference that is not a difference in kind or of genus. That is to say, for Levinas, there is an absolute gulf between myself and my neighbour that does not obtain between myself and, for example, my neighbour's cat or my neighbour's aspidistra. When it comes to myself and my neighbour's cat or aspidistra, Levinas claims that we are merely different in kind. Yet when it comes to the other person, I am faced by something absolutely other to me, a 'rupture in being' (Levinas 1981, 87). This idea of absolute otherness only makes sense if we see ourselves as being separated out from the world in a fundamental sense. If my consciousness was a whole realm entire unto itself, entirely inaccessible to others, then the difference that is encountered in the meeting of two consciousnesses could not be easily overcome. Yet if we are much more mixed and worldly things, not set apart from everything else but enmeshed in it, then the problem simply does not exist in the same way.

Harlequin Selves

My consciousness, far from being an inner sanctum separated out from the world, is irreducibly bound up with the world, a hodgepodge of fluctuating stories and multiple drafts to which even I may not have privileged access.[2] And without there being a single absolute difference, we are left instead just with differences. We are conglomerations of semi-ordered processes. Our heads are full of ideas that we have caught on the wind and that have taken up residence of their own accord, even while we foolishly claim them as our own. These bodies that we care for and nurture, that we shield from pain, consist of countless cells that go about their business with no concern for us and our fine thoughts. 'Who am I?', Serres asks, and the answer he gives does not lead inward, but instead outwards. The self, he says, is a patchwork resembling Harlequin's coat, a badly-stitched tatter, a conjunction of adjectives. The self is 'a mixed body: studded, spotted, zebrine, tigroid, shimmering, spotted like an ocelot, whose life must be its business' (Serres 1997, 145). This is a view shared by that master-storyteller, Italo Calvino, who asks who this self might be if it is not, 'a combinatoria of experiences, information, books we have read, things imagined? Each life is an encyclopaedia, a library, an inventory of objects, a series of styles, and everything can be constantly shuffled and reordered in every way conceivable'; and in this continual shuffling, the self, Calvino writes, is not separate from the world but shares 'that nature common to each and every thing' (Calvino 1996, 124).

This leads us to a very different idea of ethics from that provided by Levinas. The high drama has gone, and we are left with something rather quieter and—yes, it has to be admitted —rather more muddled. Here we are, in the thick of things, mixed and shifting selves making our way through a mixed and shifting world.

What is ethics? Let us advance a working definition. Ethics is that muddle which helps us muddle through an already muddled world. Ethics—like love, like death, like our own selves—is not a single thing; it is not something that can be captured in a single account. It is perfectly possible to admire Levinas's account of ethics, and to appreciate his phenomenological acuity, while also leaving room for other accounts and other stories that can throw a rather different light on the muddle that is ethics.

A Stroll by the River: Fish and Other Others

As I have already said, I can find no account of ethics that better describes the dynamics of that encounter in the bazaar in Darjeeling than that provided by Levinas. Yet when Levinas speaks of the other others with whom we share the world, he does so rather less successfully. Take, for example, the other others with whom we share our homes and our lives, as our ancestors have done since prehistory: *dogs*. Dogs are sometimes said to be a man's best friend; they occupy our houses and enter to some extent into social relations with us; they are endowed with names to which they answer, even if they cannot reciprocate and call us by *our* name; they even mourn our deaths (the famous Scottish mutt Greyfriars Bobby was said to have sat by his owner's grave for fourteen years) as we mourn theirs. When we say to our dog 'Good dog!', and the dog wags its tail, we have the sense that the dog knows something of goodness. When we put on our sternest face and say 'Bad dog!', the dog behaves as we would expect any miscreant to behave. So we come to a question that, on occasion, perplexes scholars of Levinas: does a dog have a face? Of course, we might say, a dog has a face. It has a wet nose, those endearing dark eyes, those cute, expressive ears. But does it have a face in the sense that Levinas means? When a group of graduate students from Warwick University visited Levinas and asked him whether his idea of the 'face' can be applied to non-human others, Levinas himself tackled the question with reference to the four-footed companions with whom so many of us share our homes:

> One cannot entirely refuse the face of an animal. It is via the face that one understands, for example, a dog. Yet the priority here is not found in the animal, but in the human face. We understand the animal, the face of an animal, in accordance with Dasein. The phenomenon of the face is not in its purest form in the dog. In the dog, in the animal, there are other phenomena. For example, the force of nature is pure vitality. It is more this which characterises the dog. But it also has a face... (Wright, Hughes et al. 1998, 169)

This is far from being an unambiguous answer to the question. It seems that if a dog *does* have a face, it only does so by proxy, understood 'in accordance with Dasein', that is, understood in accordance with human existence. It is as if Levinas is saying that a dog has a face only insofar as it can have honorary or partially human status. At this point, one would have liked the students to have risked the accusation of facetiousness by pushing the question further. Does a cat have a face? A gerbil? A woodpecker? A *fish*?

While he hedges his bets when it comes to dogs, it is hard to imagine Levinas having much time for the idea that a fish might have a face, or the idea that I could be infinitely responsible for a fish.[3] Fish, as far as we human beings are concerned, are more alien to us than the stranger who knocks on our door, or the dog who wags his tail in greeting. They move in a different element, they have no lungs, their blood is cold, not warm, they do not sleep.[4] And yet, while they may not have faces in the sense that Levinas means, they still have faces, in the ordinary everyday sense: we can look them in the eye, and these denizens of another world can look back.

It is a melancholy fact that the Western philosophical tradition has not, in general, tended to look very kindly upon fish. Philosophy has always had its eyes set upon the heights, and as a result has preferred not to investigate the seas, the rivers and the lakes. So when philosophers have gazed upon fish, they have tended to view them as creatures who have simply tried hard enough at the business of ascending towards the lofty heights where philosophers like to spend their days (or where philosophers like to imagine that they spend their days: when it comes to these two stories, you can take your pick). Plato does not have a good word to say about them. In the *Timaeus*, he discusses how the gods decide the forms in which souls are reborn.

The fourth kind of animal, the kind that lives in water, came from those men who were without question the most stupid and ignorant of all. The gods who brought about their transformation concluded that these no longer deserved to breathe pure air, because their souls were tainted with transgressions of every sort. Instead of letting them breathe rare and pure air, they shoved them into water to breathe its murky depths. This is the origin of fish, of all shellfish, and of every water-inhabiting animal. Their justly due reward for their extreme stupidity is their extreme dwelling place. (*Timaeus* 92b)

If Plato's dim view of the mental powers of fish were not bad enough, he also adds moral condemnation to his scorn. Fish are cast into the waters by the gods, he says, because of their stupidity and ignorance; and their stupidity and ignorance, in turn, reflect their moral turpitude.[5] Fish, for Plato, are not only where they are because of their ignorance and their wrong-doing, but their condition itself acts as a fitting metaphor for this ignorance:

It is as if someone who lived deep down in the middle of the ocean thought he was living on its surface. Seeing the sun and the other heavenly bodies through the water, he would think the sea to be the sky; because he is slow and weak, he has never reached the surface of the sea or risen with his head above the water or come out of the sea to our region here, nor seen how much purer and more beautiful it is than his own region, nor has he ever heard of it from anyone who has seen it.[6] (*Phaedo* 109c-d)

Fortunately, this disapproval of our finny brethren is not common to all philosophers and philosophies. Over in China, two philosophers once went for a stroll in the country, and there they contemplated the life of fishes without any hint of the kind of moral disapproval in which Plato indulged:

> Zhuangzi and Huizi had strolled onto the bridge over the Hao, when the former observed, 'See how the minnows are darting about! That is the pleasure of fishes.' 'You not being a fish yourself,' said Huizi, 'how can you possibly know in what consists the pleasure of fishes?' 'And you not being I,' retorted Zhuangzi, 'how can you know that I do not know?' 'If I, not being you, cannot know what you know,' urged Huizi, 'it follows that you, not being a fish, cannot know in what consists the pleasure of fishes.' 'Let us go back,' said Zhuangzi, 'to your original question. You asked me how I knew in what consists the pleasure of fishes. Your very question shows that you knew I knew. I knew it from my own feelings on the bridge.' (O'Flaherty 1990, 77)[7]

This is a passage that is not entirely unknown within the Western philosophical tradition. Heidegger was particularly fond of this story, having read from it at a seminar on empathy and intersubjectivity in 1930 (Parkes 1987, 105).[8] The story suggests that the question of solipsism—how do I, not being you, know what you know (or that you know at all)—is in the end nonsensical. The two sages are in a conversation, and this presupposes that they both accept that the other has knowledge. But what makes this story interesting is that the possibilities of this intersubjective and empathetic identification are extended beyond the two interlocutors to the fish in the pool. *Of course* the fish are having fun down there in the pool, *of course* there is pleasure in swimming as there is pleasure in walking across the bridge. We know this, from our feelings on the bridge as we watch them going about their business.[9]

Doniger points out in her reflections upon this story that the sages nevertheless remain sages and the fish, fish. The story is about a kind of empathic understanding by virtue of which I can know another while remaining securely myself and while the other remains securely other. Such empathy may be useful and necessary, but as we know from the stories woven by Levinas, we cannot reduce our relationships with others—even with fishy others—to empathy. But if the ancient Chinese sages seem to be occupying one extreme—the view from the bridge —the opposite extreme is occupied by the Indian sage Saubhari, who apparently meditated for twelve years totally immersed in a pool of water. At first, his meditations were unshakeable, but before too long he started to notice the fish in the pond. In particular, his attention was taken by a great-grandfather fish with innumerable children, grandchildren and great-grandchildren, and he saw that the great-grandfather fish was living happily amongst his descendants. Seeing this, the sage began to envy the fish and to wish for children of his own. So he got out of the water, went to the king, married all fifty of the king's daughters, begot three children by each one of his wives and, realising at long last that the desire for reproduction was self-perpetuating—there was no point at which it would reach a natural terminus, it fuelled itself, the children kept on coming—he abandoned the palace, his spouses and his many offspring, and went back to meditate in the forest. The sage's mistake, says Doniger, was in 'believing that he personally can be happy like a fish, or rather that such happiness is desirable for him: he comes to learn that though other people may be like fish, he himself is not like them...' (O'Flaherty 1990, .78-9). It could be said that both extremes—on the one hand a form of empathy in which nothing is at stake for us, an empathy in which there's really nothing much at risk for us, and on the other hand the desire to throw our lot in and to become entirely other than we are—commit the same error in seeing the self and the other as entirely distinct categories. Doniger suggests a third option: the possibility of leading an amphibious, which is to say mixed, existence such that we might be able to exist both within the water and on dry land, a possibility that lies between the dream of finally becoming a fish, and the safety of our sagely musings on the bank. Perhaps we are, when it comes down to it, neither sages nor fish, but are instead amphibious creatures whose fate—and whose glory— is to inhabit many worlds.

The Prophetic Speech of Fish

We are, however, uneasy with the idea of an amphibious existence. We aspire, like good heirs of Plato, to sagehood, and pretend to ourselves that we have little in common with the fish whom we watch from the bank-side. Yet as we stand there engaged in sagely debate about the lives of fish or the virtues of entering the water, it sometimes happens that a fish of peculiar talents decides to engage us on our own terms, itself becoming amphibious for a moment, and entering our own world where it plays havoc with all of our certainties. Fish do not often take the trouble to chat with us, and when they do, what they say frequently has a kind of urgency to it. Out of the blue, the fish appears. It speaks with us to advise or to warn. And then it falls silent. Fish are admirable creatures in at least one respect: they do not waste their words.

Talking fish are common in folk tales the world over; but there is, I cannot help feeling, something particularly uncanny about a *fish* that talks. A talking fish is much more unsettling than a talking dog or a talking cat. The more sentimental or the more paranoid amongst us may well suspect that, as a matter of course, cats spend their time casting coolly critical gazes over us as we go about our daily business, forming opinions and making judgements. When we fall prey to these suspicions, we may also find ourselves thinking darkly that the only reason these creatures do not talk to us is that they do not have the machinery—or, perhaps, the inclination—to do so. A talking cat, in other words, is just an ordinary, everyday cat: but an ordinary, everyday cat endowed with either the machinery for speaking or the wish to speak. But fish are different. They occupy a world that we imagine to be silent.[10] It would take more than the machinery and the will for them to speak, it would take a third thing. The fish would have to be exceptional amongst fish not only in that it could speak nor only in that it wished to speak, but also—and here we may be simply showing that our old Platonic prejudices are still intact—in that it *had something to say*. It is, then, perhaps no wonder that we bank-side sages do not have a particularly good track record when it comes to our conversations with fish, as the following two stories—one from New York, and the other once again from the Tanimbar islands—will demonstrate.

On 15th March 2003, the *New York Times* reported the following tale. In New York's New Square fish market, a fish—a twenty-pound carp—opened its mouth and spoke to Luis Nivelo, an Ecuadorian immigrant. Mr Nivelo was so terrified that he collapsed into a pile of packing crates before running to alert his colleague, a Hasidic Jew called Zalmen Rosen.

Mr Rosen arrived on the scene to hear the fish saying 'Tzaruch shemirah' and 'Hasof bah,' which he translated as meaning 'everyone needs to account for themselves because the end is nigh.' The fish went on to say that it was the reincarnated soul of a local Hasidic man who had died the year before, and instructed Mr Rosen to study the Torah and to pray. Unfortunately, in his panic, Mr Rosen became momentarily deranged and attempted to kill the fish. Mr Nivelo, not speaking Hebrew and convinced that the fish was a devil, joined in. Before long, the fish lay dead on the slab, silent. It was sold, cooked and eaten.[11]

One can hardly blame Mr Rosen for losing his head and bludgeoning the prophetic fish to death: these are some situations in life for which nothing can prepare us. It is not necessary even to understand what the fish is saying to be amazed by the spectacle of a fish that talks. Luis Nivelo, who spoke no Hebrew, was sufficiently horrified to collapse; and Mr Rosen, despite the fact that the fish was giving him what seemed like important information and guidance in a language that he understood well, nevertheless did not have the presence of mind to stop and listen. So much for the fish from New York. But let us now go back to the Tanimbar islands for our second story, one that was told to me in the village of Alusi Batjasi, and that reinforces the point that fish, when they speak to us, often do so to warn prophetically, and that when they do, those to whom they speak often pay scant regard.

Once, the story goes, there had been no buffalo in Tanimbar. At this time, there was a young man of low birth. One day he was walking on the shore and he saw a girl fishing on the reef with a spear. She was beautiful, adorned with richly-coloured *ikat* cloth,[12] the daughter of a noble family. The two of them spoke and fell in love. Knowing that the girl's parents would never give their consent to the match, they decided to elope into the forest.

On the appointed night, the young man crept up to the maiden's house. Noble houses in those days were raised on stilts to keep out snakes, rats and other vermin, the entrance being up a short ladder, through a trap-door. The young man crept under the house and called softly to the girl. His beloved, who had not slept a wink out of fear that she might miss him, lifted the trap-door and descended the ladder to where he was waiting. They took each other's hands, their path lit only by the light of a full moon, and they stole deep into the forest, on fire with passionate longing.

Eventually, they came upon a beautiful glade. The grass was soft and in the centre of the clearing a pool of dark water reflected the moon. The two lovers walked to the bank. The water looked clear and cool. With trembling hands, they stripped off each other's clothes until they stood pale and naked in the moonlight.

Just as they were about to leap into the water, out of the pool jumped a fish with a loud *plop!* The fish did not, as is usual, fall back into the water, but remained hanging in mid-air, fixing them both with a beady and supercilious glare. The couple stood open-mouthed. Then the fish spoke.

'Do not bathe in this pool,' said the fish, 'It is a sacred pool, and you'll only regret it if you do.'

With this piece of advice, the fish fell back into the water with another *plop!* and was gone. The lovers looked at each other, hesitating for a moment; but who has ever heeded the advice of a fish? What counsel, however wise, will turn the hearts of lovers in the heat of their passion? The couple joined hands and plunged into the water. As soon as the water touched their skin, they felt their pale young bodies begin to blacken and swell. Their skin seemed to be thickening, turning leathery. They felt their snouts pushing forwards and growing in size. Their arms and legs started to change shape, and from the bases of their spines, tails began to protrude. Their breath became ill-smelling and rasping, and from their temples emerged pointed horns. The lovers tried to cry out in horror, but the only sound that came from their mouths was a hollow bellowing.

The two buffalo stood in the pool, snorting in bewilderment. They climbed out on to the bank to stand, dripping and confused, in the glade. Taking no notice of their discarded clothing lying on the ground, with a flick of their tails they turned and trotted into the forest.

This Ovidian tale from the southern hemisphere may seem sad, although the sadness is alleviated by the knowledge that the young couple did indeed find the fulfilment of that passion which had brought them to the forest. These two buffalo, it is said, were the ancestors of every single buffalo in the whole of the Tanimbar islands; and to this day it is well known that to disturb a pair of amorous buffalo in the heat of copulation is to court disaster.

When fish talk, it seems, their words are worth heeding. Both the carp in the New York fish market and the Tanimbarese fish bring to the human protagonists of the stories a knowledge that they themselves could not possibly have possessed. But when a fish speaks in Hebrew, it becomes apparent that we must move beyond Levinas to be able to think adequately about these other others with whom we share our world.[13] If these fish are, in a sense, prophetic, they do not descend from the heights to speak to us. Instead, they either emerge from the depths or else they cross over from one world to another. The knowledge that they bring us is not higher knowledge, but knowledge of a different world. The passage that they make so that they can speak to us is not one of transcendence and ascent, but rather of traversal and crossing-over. In these moments in which it becomes possible for the human protagonists of our stories to speak with fish, we are dealing with an encounter with otherness that is utterly different in nature from anything dreamed of by Levinas. The fish do not just transfer bulletins, packets of information, from one world to another. Instead, these brave creatures, in the moment of their exposure cut a passage between different worlds, and as they do so, new and surprising knowledge arises. It has to be said that this crossing-over is a risky business. The prophetic fish from Alusi Batjasi falls back into the water unscathed, but the garrulous carp from New York finds itself bludgeoned to death on a slab. The dangers are the same in the passage in the other direction when, against all advice, the young Tanimbarese lovers cross over into the water and thereby become changed for good.

The misfortunes of the New York carp and of the Tanimbarese lovers should remind us that in encounters with strangeness and otherness, everything may be at stake. This is an ordinary, everyday experience. When we immerse ourselves in stories that are not our own stories, in ideas that are not our own ideas, in languages that are not our own languages, amongst peoples who are not our own peoples, we find that we are moving into an alien element. We lose all reference as ungraspable floods of information pour around us, buffeting us first here, then there. In experiences such as this, a kind of infinity of possibility begins to open, an infinity that is not—as it is in Levinas—anything to do with transcendence, but is instead to do with the opening of a multitude of new traversals, crossings, translations and displacements. As we enter the water, and if we do not sink utterly, we find ourselves surrendering to these fluctuating tides. The certainties to which we had once grasped—the self-certainty that Levinas claims tends to dull us to the living needs of others, the moral certainty that, unfounded as it is, leads to rancour, disputate and warfare— may begin to subside. Not knowing where or who or what we are, we start to swim...

Traversal, Not Transcendence

The desert, too, is a shifting sea, with its navigators and its curiously swaying ships, its depths and its currents. And so there I am, or my previous self, swathed in a blanket and sitting on a bus that is driving by night through the desert. As I glance out of the window, the lights of a town appear in the distance. Figuig, on the Algerian border. It is dark, and half the travellers are asleep. That these lights might—very soon—resolve into precisely this hotel where I will sleep tonight, precisely this café where I will eat, precisely this street down which I shall walk seems, here swaddled in the dark of the passage, almost impossible.

There is something beautiful about coming upon an unknown town in the desert at night, a beauty that is not without a taste of threat or of danger. Between towns, between sleep and waking, the lights continue to glimmer on the horizon. A breathtaking constellation, a galaxy. The bus jolts and one of the passengers awakens with a cry before falling asleep again. Somebody is smoking a cigarette at the back of the bus. The burning end glows red in the dark. I gaze out of the window. It may not look like it, but I am swimming for my life.

There is so much movement. Ever since emerging out of Africa, *Homo sapiens* have restlessly traversed the face of the Earth along the filaments and nets of interlocking pathways, trails and tracks. Europe, the Middle East, Asia, by boat to Australia; northwards and across the Bering Strait, south again through North America, South America, Tierra del Fuego. The skies are traced with endless spiderweb filaments. Wanderlust afflicts us: from Tiznit to Tafraoute; from Tafraoute to Figuig; from Figuig to Ouarzazate. Creeping across the face of the globe in buses, cars, on foot, in airplanes that—despite all appearances of height—merely hug the earth's surface, seven miles up, no higher than the distance to the next town or village, or a couple of hours' walk. We are in motion, in-between. Amid all these multiple passages, it is not a matter of seeking a single transcendent principle, but rather of attuning ourselves to the complexity of which we are a part. Bruce Chatwin writes,

> *Le Désert est monothéiste.* Renan's aphorising implies that blank horizons and a dazzling sky will clear the mind of its distractions and allow it to concentrate on the Godhead. But life in the desert is not like that! To survive at all, the desert dweller—Tuareg or Aboriginal—must develop a prodigious sense of orientation. He must forever be naming, sifting, comparing a thousand different 'signs'—the tracks of a dung beetle or the ripple of a dune—to tell him where he is; where the others are; where rain has fallen; where the next meal is coming from; whether if plant X is in flower, plant Y will be in berry, and so forth. (Chatwin 1998, 100)[14]

So we move through endless signs and encounters and meetings, restless and uncalm. The only complete calm is in death. In this world of endless dispersal, there is no single anchor-point, no absolute difference or absolute sameness that we can grasp. Difference spreads everywhere, like the ripples in a pond, through us and around us. We return to ourselves again and again, and find ourselves different. We are feverish translators: Arabic into French; French into English; your world into mine; the world of the fish into the world of the human; the world of the human into the world of the fish; what we were into what we are; what we are into what we will be. Moving horizontally, not vertically, through a thousand traversals, not transcendences. We become familiar with first this, then that. We leave ourselves behind on the road, and we take ourselves with us. We translate ourselves into ourselves, constantly, through the stories that we weave, through the conversations we have with others. 'If you cud even jus see 1 thing clear the woal of whats in it you cud see every thing clear,' writes Russell Hoban in *Riddley Walker*. 'But you never wil get to see the woal of any thing youre all ways in the middl of it living it or moving thru it' (Hoban 2002, 186). We never see every thing clear. We never see every thing clouded. We see in half-light, in shadow and in light. We are all ways in the middl of it living it or moving thru it.

The bus arrives at Figuig and those passengers who were asleep wake, either through the jostling of their neighbours or because they have become aware that the rhythmic movement of the bus has come to a halt. Outside there are voices, and each voice is a possibility, several possibilities, countless possibilities. I struggle to my feet and lurch into the warm night. '*Bonsoir*,' says a voice from out of the dark. I turn and smile.

Restlessness

In the opening pages of *Totality and Infinity*, Levinas describes his metaphysical quest in terms of restlessness. *Metaphysics*, he writes,

> is turned toward the 'elsewhere' and the 'otherwise' and the 'other.' For in the most general form it has assumed in the history of thought it appears as a movement going forth from a world that is familiar to us, whatever be the yet unknown lands that bound it or that it hides from view, from an 'at home' which we inhabit, toward an alien outside-of-oneself, toward a yonder. (Levinas 1969, 33)

But why should this restless movement be a movement upward? Why can it not be a movement outward? Not transcendence but traversal. Levinas's own answer to this question hinges upon the distinction he draws between desire and need.

Need, he writes, is a hunger for that which can be absorbed into our own identity, that upon which I can 'feed' and make my own. Desire, however, cannot be sated, it is never satisfied. I can eat bread, and it can become a part of me. I can learn a poem, and it can become a part of me also. But metaphysical desire, this nagging desire for an 'elsewhere' cannot be sated. It is not a desire for an object which I can absorb.[15] However, if we no longer have the possibility of absolute difference, and if the self is indeed a tattered Harlequin patchwork, then the distinction between desire and need starts to collapse. There on the bus through the desert, between past and future, between the point of departure and the arrival, a patchwork of dreams and hopes and fears and impressions, bits of conversation half-remembered or half-imagined, there is an encounter with otherness that cannot be well described either in terms of Levinas's 'need' for that which I can absorb into my own being, or in terms of his 'desire' for that which is absolutely different.[16] The recognition of restlessness simply does not require the extravagant metaphysical conclusions that Levinas draws. What is the engine that drives our restlessness, if it is not simply our harlequin nature? We are unquiet selves, restless until death. And at those times that we feel that we are reaching states close to that of equilibrium, we would do well to remember that such stability can last only for a short duration, while conditions permit; before long, we are teetering off in new directions, out of balance, heading off on a new course.

The Otherness of Stories

And so we return to the telling of stories, because in this continual traversal and translation, this endless mixing, stories are not only the means we use to orientate ourselves, but they are also themselves fresh traversals, translations and passages.

Later that night in Figuig, having washed off the dust of the journey and found some food to eat, I find myself sitting by a brazier, or else at a table in a small café. And there, with the night kept at bay by scarce light of the fire or of the fluctuating bulb that hangs from the ceiling, I trade tales with strangers, as the travellers do in Calvino's dream-city of Euphemia.

> You do not come to Euphemia only to buy and sell, but also because at night, by the fires all around the market, seated on sacks or barrels or stretched out on piles of carpets, at each word that one man says—such as 'wolf,' 'sister,' 'hidden treasure,' 'battle,' 'scabies,' 'lovers'—the others tell, each one, his tale of wolves, sisters, treasures, scabies, lovers, battles. And you know that in the long journey ahead of you, when to keep awake against the camel's swaying or the junk's rocking, you start summoning up your memories one by one, your wolf will have become another wolf, you sister a different sister, your battle other battles, on your return from Euphemia, the city where memory is traded at every solstice and at every equinox. (Calvino 1997, 36-7)

In this trading of tales, experience itself is transformed. My bus becomes another bus, the cigarette glowing in the darkness and the constellation of the town's lights, another cigarette and another constellation. For we do not own our stories, they are not our possessions. We cannot incorporate them fully as Levinas claims we can incorporate those things that we need. They slip away from us even as we tell them. And so we trade them, for they only live in the telling; but as we do so, they inevitably become the stories of others, other to the stories that they themselves once were. Similarly, as others tell us their stories, so our own stories become different to how they once were, such that our memories, our battles, our wolves, our sisters, even our scabies—should we be so unfortunate as to have scabies—become altered.

In this telling of tales, I do not entirely lose the story that I pass on; but neither do I keep hold of it in the same fashion as before. There is a gain and a loss. Both are inevitable, and a strict accounting of the two is impossible. Even if I sit in silence and listen to the stories of others, although at first glance it may seem that in the hearing I only make gains, there are also losses, subtle losses: as I hear about another's sister—perhaps about her expertise in cooking aubergines— my own sister seems a greater or lesser aubergine cook than before; when I am told about the wolf, the traveller to my side once encountered on a lonely hillside, the wolf with which I exchanged glances one day in the municipal zoo transforms into a different wolf; and through these subtle, perhaps imperceptible changes in my sister or my wolf, so too I am changed.

To tell our stories is to transform them, to transform ourselves, to unstitch and restitch Harlequin's cape; and to listen to the stories of others is not only to permit these stories to be transformed in the telling, nor only to permit ourselves to be transformed in ways that we may not be able to gauge, in ways that we may be unable to either anticipate or recollect, but it is also to subject our own stories to transformation. This is why we cannot see those prophetic fish as merely conveying bounded packets of information from one world to another. This trading of tales is more than the movement of bald tokens between different accounts.

Stories, then, are not merely about others, but in their own character as passages and traversals, they themselves are movements through and towards otherness. 'So stories are travels,' Rebecca Solnit writes in her exploration of the wanderlust and restlessness that afflict us, 'and travels are stories' (Solnit 2000, 72). Like a sailor adrift in a small raft, when we are cast off on the tides of a story, we find that not only are we borne through another element—a milieu that is itself other to the supposedly dry ground of our reasons and our philosophies—but also that we wash up elsewhere, an elsewhere that cannot be predicted.

Otherness, Novelty, Passages Elsewhere

We cannot say, 'through the telling of this story you will come to understand proposition x,' nor can we say, 'this story will cause an increase in compassion in the hearer.' The story may do these things, but it may do other things altogether. Why else do moralists love to append didactic aphorisms to the end of stories, if not out of a secret fear of this 'elsewhere'? The otherness of a story is more than a matter of its content; instead, it lies in the fact of it being a story at all. The story is other to us—even if we know it well, even if we have learned every word by heart—in that it continually threatens to launch new wanderings, further passages. It is not just that our stories are *often* about others: sages and Gods, fish and saints. It is not just a simple case of stories teaching us, by conveying information to us, what otherness is like. Even the best-known, most familiar story quivers with possibilities of newness. Again and again, Kierkegaard's pseudonymous author journeys with Abraham; each time the same, each time different. There could be more retellings, an infinity of retellings, were there sufficient time, and still we would not exhaust the story.

We can imagine a story, then, as a message in a bottle cast off from the shore. The bottle is laid gently in the water and sucked out to sea by the receding tide. What now will happen? We can perhaps make some predictions as to where the bottle may wind up, but these—at very best—are probabilistic rather than certain. It may be that the bottle is improperly sealed, that it will take in water and sink, becoming the home of a hermit crab. It may cross the Atlantic, or drift down to the southern ocean and eventually, by who knows what currents, wash up on the shores of Australia. It may return to the hither shore at the next high tide. Now imagine a second bottle cast upon the waters in exactly the same way at exactly the same time. Would it follow the same course as the first? Almost certainly not. Is the course completely determined? Perhaps. There is no way of telling, because we will never, out there in the world, be confronted with just this situation. We cannot step into the same river twice. We cannot cast off the same bottle from the same shore at the same time more than once. Determined or not, the movement of the bottle remains unpredictable. If we do introduce a second bottle, it cannot be in precisely the same position as the first. Perhaps we cast them off alongside each other, in which case it seems unlikely they will reach the same destination. The conditions under which those two bottles are acting will not be identical. If we do not displace the second bottle in space, we can displace it in time and cast it off a few moments later from the very same spot, or the following morning, or the same time next year: but we will still face the same problem of indeterminacy. There is no perfect replication of any set of conditions anywhere in the universe, not unless Nietzsche's dream of recurrence is discovered—one day through the grinding necessity of all that is—to be more than a dream.[17] Whether the second bottle is set adrift at the same time, but displaced in terms of space, or set adrift at the same place, but displaced in terms of time, the conditions each bottle will be subject to are different.

For Levinas, the only possibility of true novelty is in the face of the other, the stranger who knocks on the door. Levinas's ethics requires transcendence to bring us novelty, or an escape from the monotony of the same old thing. But this movement of transcendence, although it promises something new, seems to never deliver on its promise. To move in the direction of transcendence is always to move away from plurality and towards unity. Plato dreams of the sun as an image of goodness and unity; Kant dreams of transcendental conditions that stand outside of the hubbub of the world; and Levinas dreams of the good that shines from the face of another that saves us from the interminable, rumbling horror of existence. But these dreams are always dreams of the same old thing. In the story that Levinas is telling, although we may encounter newness in the face of the other, when it comes down to it, it is always the same novelty.

Ethics—this great, bewildering muddle of good-will and hope and confusion and false certainty—is, if it is about anything at all, surely about more than the endless reiteration of the same old novelty. We are indeed strange and wonderful creatures. In continual flux, quivering with uncertainty, hopelessly tangled up in the world, with little prospect of redemption here and now, let alone in any world beyond, frenetically spinning tales and yarns that weave and unweave fragile webs of understanding and misunderstanding. The story that Levinas tells of the face is not the only ethical story that can be told. When we finally recognise the muddle that is ethics for what it really is, then we are able to ask about the other imperatives that are woven into our experience, imperatives that we may have hitherto overlooked. What imperatives might we encounter in our relationships with beings such as these: mountains, images, wolves, scabies, sages, princesses, woodpeckers, stories, truths, buffalo, forests, cities, strangers, friends, lovers, fish, seas? What stories might we use to describe them? For these things, too, demand our attention, and perhaps also our response.

Death, love, ethics... perhaps none of these are single things. But then, why should they be? We ourselves are not single things. And this recognition alone may enable us to open the door to a consideration of a wider range of stories, to a greater breadth of data, than the philosophers have often allowed. It may even do more than this. It may, at the same time, be sufficient to deprive our ethical convictions of at least a

little of their rigidity and force, so that we can begin to recognise again the perplexity that simmers beneath our attempts to
think through ethics. And in this way, perhaps, we might be
able to begin to find new ways in which our mutual enmities
and disputes may be eased.

9

CONCLUSION: BEYOND DREAMS OF DRY LAND

The dream is over, wrote Husserl. The hope that philosophy might have delivered us into a safe harbour, somewhere where we can escape the winds and the tides, has come to nothing. One more prophet disappears overboard, and we find ourselves standing on deck, scanning the horizon that extends in all directions until our eyes and our hearts ache with longing—but there is nothing on the horizon other than the blurred haze where the sky and sea meet.

If philosophy has failed in delivering us from this life afloat in the endless seas of existence without any certainties with which to anchor ourselves, then it should be granted that there is at least the *possibility* this failure is not a necessary one. Who knows? Perhaps even Husserl was not rigorous enough in his methods; or perhaps he simply took a wrong course and another, greater, navigator will one day take the ship's wheel and bring us to the dreamed-of haven. Then at last, after all this time, it may be possible for us to found the kind of moral community of which Husserl dreamed, a community based upon the infinite goals of reason.

Yet there is good reason to be sceptical of such dreams, dreams that even Husserl eventually despaired of ever being realised. And there is good reason to think that, in giving up on such dreams, we need not abandon all hope of speaking meaningfully about ethics. There is a course that can be steered between dreams of solid ground on the one hand and the cycles of endless equivocation on the other. My aim here has not been to seize the ship's wheel and to turn it about, setting a course to a safe harbour. Instead, it has been merely to recognise that these prophets, although they have dreamed impossible dreams, have nevertheless not been without insight. I have attempted to do justice to at least some of these insights, without giving in to dreams of dry land, or losing an attentiveness to the winds and the tides that pass to and fro across the ocean of stories. And by means of this attention, I hope that I may have eased to some extent the hydrophobic shuddering that sees, in these endless waters, nothing but the endlessly rolling darkness. I did not promise dry land at the outset, so it should come as no surprise that we are no closer to a safe harbour than we were at the outset. What I can offer, in lieu of a firm conclusion, is a handful of naïve suggestions.

Firstly, I would suggest that ethics seems to need phenomenology—an attentiveness to experience, to the question 'what is *x* like?' It is precisely this kind of attentiveness that philosophy has tended to overlook, preferring to deal with abstract cases rather than real-world navigation.

Secondly, one of the best (and certainly the most well-established) methods of phenomenology that we have is that of storytelling.

Thirdly, to understand how stories work, we need to understand them in the plural rather than in the singular, we need to understand that stories ebb and flow like the sea.

When we appreciate this, and when we give up our aspirations to find *the* story, the Ur-text that can be foundational for all others, then we can see, fourthly, that storytelling, as a mode of thinking born out of attentiveness, leads us away from the kinds of thinking that the philosophers have favoured. Through telling stories, we find that we ourselves are more sea-like—more multiple, more unstable, more changing—than the philosophers have tended to credit.

Fifthly—to return to the passage in Plato's early dialogue, the *Euthyphro*—the problem presented by the absence of ethical agreement may perhaps be best responded to not by finding some key that may once and for all resolve our differences, but conversely by the recognition that ethics is born out of differences such as these, and is more about moving between and within stories and uncertainties, with all the kindness, patience and care that we can muster.

And finally, perhaps, it would be worth adding that, amid all this flux and uncertainty, anyone worth their salt would make use of the best shared knowledge there is available, knowledge of the world and of ourselves. Good navigators are also good empiricists, and so perhaps ethics requires not merely a close phenomenological attention to the nuances of experience—the subject of this book—but also an appreciation of what the sciences, the ordinary, everyday, painstaking, empirical sciences, have to tell us about what it is to be human.

This, then, may serve as a sketch of some of the things that may be useful components of a worldly approach to ethics, an approach to ethics that gives up on dreams of transcendence. Cast adrift at the moment of our birth, we are constant voyagers. The horizon stretches on in all directions, as it always has done, without sight of dry land. The waves, sometimes calm and sometimes in uproar, knock tirelessly against the side of the ship. The prophets, for all of their hope and their goodness, have not yet seen their prophecies fulfilled. There are times when we are clinging on to the sides of the boat for dear life, and we cry out for some kind of Messiah. Yet the Messiah does not come, the storms inevitably pass, and if we are fortunate enough, or cunning enough, or sturdy enough, we survive a little longer. 'We ourselves,' Michel Serres writes, 'born from the vortices, like naked Aphrodite in the foaming seas, are troublemakers full of troubles':

> I can do nothing about the vortex that brought my birth, and whose unfolding will bring my death. The science of time, that of things and of the world, teaches me that existence is disorder and disordered destruction. Through it, my time escapes me and death is near. Wisdom: avoid adding more movement to the vortex, to that which carries off the dense elements of the body, which screws down or enfolds the subtle elements of the soul. Halt the cyclone, try to escape it. Quell the disorder: ataraxy. (Serres 2000, 90)

This has been a naïve kind of voyage and has taken us a long way from sober philosophical climes. We have travelled alongside the kind of motley company that many philosophers would prefer to shun; and for some, the lack of any final landfall will still come as a disappointment, even though I have repeatedly promised none. The bad news is this: that there is no way out, and that we are all heading, whether we like it or not, for watery graves. But why the long face? After all, there is good news as well. In this space in between, we find that there is a chance to live, and to respond to those demands upon us, to those imperatives that speak to us, that bear on us from all different directions and in all kinds of fashions, imperatives that speak to us not out of some terrifying abyss of absolute difference, but simply because we are irredeemably tangled up in the world, a part of things, unable to extract ourselves from all of these thousand thousand shimmering threads. And perhaps this is not the intolerable burden that we might fear, but instead something that offers the possibility of joy, these multitudinous threads linking us to the world, to many worlds, endless pathways that can draw us back from the aridity in which we all too often imprison ourselves, to the point at which we can again recognise—breathing the sea air deeply into our chests—that there is nowhere to go, outside of all of these relationships, tangled though they may be.

But now it is late, and the moon is rising over the rooftops, or over the waves. Perhaps your eyelids are closing as if of their own accord, or the book is weighing heavy in your hand. Sometimes, as I have already said, sleep is better than philosophy. So let me finish with a story and wish you good night. The story goes like this...

One day, aboard ship, I was standing on deck debating with the philosophers and the prophets. I had been there since noon, and we were all hot and bothered. The dialectic was subtle, the logic glittering, the arguments on all sides brilliant. But nobody could agree. I myself was struggling to keep up. I was tired, with the beginnings of a headache.

I saw the second mate approach, a quiet man, unschooled and softly-spoken, and I nodded in greeting. I didn't know him well. Keeping his distance from the little group of disputants amongst whom I was numbered, he beckoned to me with a smile. Apologising to my peers, I went to speak with him. To tell the truth, I was relieved, glad that he had rescued me from these combative sages, from my own unruly love of argument. 'Fancy a drink?' he asked.

'That,' I said, 'would be great.'

He led me to the foredeck where he poured me a glass of

whisky, and one for himself. We reclined in deckchairs, looking out to sea, soaking up the rays of the late afternoon sun.

'I will tell you,' he said, 'everything that I know.'

I glanced at him but did not say a word. The sun was brilliant and red. I took a sip of my drink.

'Study the winds and the tides,' he told me. 'Quell the disorder as far as possible. Steer clear from cyclones if you are able. Do not struggle against the elements. Befriend them if you can.'

AFTERWORD TO THE REVISED EDITION

This is a book of fluid metaphors, one that attempts to tell some compelling stories about the fluidity of experience, of selves, and of the world as a whole. And so perhaps it should not be a surprise that my own positions have shifted slightly since when this book was first published: I am not quite the same person as the person who wrote this book, and the world into which it was launched is no longer quite the same world.

This was always an oddball book, one that was never really at home in the realms of academic philosophy. Several years ago, a friend told me that there were two kinds of philosophy: the kind that Kant did, and the kind that her grandmother did. 'Your kind of philosophy,' she said, 'is closer to the second kind than to the first.' I was outraged and offended, of course. But then she reassured me that in when it came to the business of *living*, she had found her grandmother's counsel far more useful than anything cooked up by the great Prussian sage.

Looking back, it is clear that she was right: I have always been far more interested in what Walter Benjamin calls 'counsel woven into the fabric of real life' than in academic debates. And *Finding Our Sea-Legs* is far less a contribution to academic philosophy (I no longer frequent the academy; I have other fish to fry—or to talk with) than it is an attempt to navigate through a bunch of perplexities to find, in the heart of these perplexities, a measure of good counsel, and a sense of a way forward.

Arguably, *Sea-Legs* is a book that is better at raising questions than it is at answering them. The questions it raises—about whether ethics may be not so much the solution to our problems as their source, about the tangled nature of experience and of our very selves, about how stories may help us make sense of the world, about how to navigate uncertainty with as much kindness and wisdom as we can muster—still preoccupy me. As for the answers the book comes to (such that they are), they are not so much philosophical propositions as they are rules-of-thumb, nuggets of folk-wisdom, proposals that may or may not turn out to be fruitful, and suggestions to go that-a-way. I cannot escape the feeling that there is much more to be said here than I have said in these pages; but then, my approach to these questions has always been more home-spun and grandmotherly than Kantian: for me the major questions have never been questions of academic philosophy (what a strange business *that* is!), but instead questions about life, and how we are to live it.

There are things that I would change, were I setting out to write this book afresh. *Sea-Legs* is a short and somewhat breathless book, and I would probably strive to move with a little more caution, to give a bit more nuance to some of the hair-raising philosophical recklessness that crops up here and there in the text—although, having said this, I do not know whether this would make for a better or worse book. Is this is a commendable and philosophically responsible impulse? Or it is instead a sign of loss of nerve? It is very hard to say.

Other things, too, seem more troubling in retrospect. One question of which I am far more aware than before is that of the gendered nature of the philosophical traditions upon which I am drawing, as well as of the language and the story-telling in this book. All those kings and princesses! As if we haven't all had enough of stories about kings and princesses... I have made a few tweaks here and there to adjust the worst instances of this, but to really address these issues would need so much reengineering that this wouldn't be a new edition so much as a new book.

Finally, there are questions of shifts in my own philosoph-ical perspectives. My commitments these days are less Buddhist than they were in the past; and a decade or more of reading Chinese philosophy has eroded some of my faith in the Indo-European philosophical traditions of which both Greek and Indian Buddhist thought are a part.

I have a strong hunch that some of the perplexities in this book might be fruitfully resolved by drawing on the resources of East Asian indigenous traditions. One thing in particular stands out as problematic, and that is the link between ethics and drama— something that is not only remarkably pronounced in the thought of Emmanuel Levinas, but also very deeply rooted in most of the traditions upon which this book draws. Although I ended the book ten years ago by talking about quelling disorder, steering clear of cyclones, and refusing the struggle against the elements, in retrospect, my commitment to this enterprise seems to have been only partial: much of the argument of this book is still caught in the trap of seeing ethics in fundamentally dramatic terms.

Against this view, I increasingly think that one of the most fruitful tasks when it comes to how we think through ethics, and human life in general, may be a wholesale de-escalation of drama. This hang-up with drama as somehow necessary to the ways in which we think through ethics strikes me as something that is neither universal, nor particularly helpful; and the resources of other philosophical traditions, in particular those of East Asia, may help thinking through questions of ethics beyond this ancient hang-up with drama.[1]

But once again, that would be another book, one that I may or may not get round to writing. So rather than allowing philosophy to have the last word, I will end with a story. And then I will leave things at that.

It was one late afternoon in autumn, and the marshes were empty.

We walked in silence towards the creek, listening to the clatter of halyards beating against aluminium masts. Under our arms were orange lifejackets. I felt a tremor of apprehension: I have never been a strong swimmer.

We crossed wooden bridges to where the boat was tethered, tied to a stake driven into the marsh. We prepared the boat quickly, our bare feet sinking into the mud. We lifted the mast and secured it in place, we unfurled the sails, then we pushed the boat out into the deep water and jumped in. I pulled the sheet tight, and the mainsail filled with wind. The jib fluttered for a moment and then swelled. We scudded across the narrow channel, I pushed the tiller away, and the boat turned towards the open water.

We picked up speed as we hit our first waves. Away from the land, the breeze was stronger, and we were moving at a good pace. We drank in the silence: the wind, the calls of the terns overhead, the slap of waves on the bows. On the starboard side, the surface of the water broke. A pair of gentle, intelligent eyes peered at us. A soft snout, a smooth forehead.

'Seal,' you said.

The seal watched us for a few seconds before it dived back into the dark water.

After an hour, maybe two, the sun was sinking towards the horizon. We began to shiver with cold, and turned the boat back towards the creek.

But when we looked towards the land, there was no longer anything to see. The autumn tides had overflowed the salt-flats. The marshes were gone. The entire world, once so substantial, was become liquid. And as darkness crept across the sky, the surface of a new-born sea glimmered with all the colours of the sunset...

ACKNOWLEDGMENTS

For Rosenzweig, true philosophy is a matter of 'speech thinking': storytelling, conversation and communal singing. I cannot claim that much in the way of communal singing went into the writing of this book, but I would like to thank some of those who shared their time and their stories, and with whom I have enjoyed the many fascinating conversations without which the book would have been a rather different one.

The philosophy department at Staffordshire University, where this book was first conceived, is as close as it gets to an Epicurean garden. I am grateful to David Webb and Helen Chapman for their wise, thoughtful and good-humoured guidance through earlier drafts of this book, to Douglas Burnham for his enormous philosophical knowledge and his excellent home-roast coffee, and to Adonis Frangeskou for his knowledge of Husserl and his philosophical fire.

Back in the early days, Toby Smith taught me a great deal about the delights of philosophy, and over the years Nagapriya Wright has been a knowledgeable and stimulating interlocutor. Thanks should also go to Wojciech Małecki, who brought my attention to Curtius's work on navigational metaphors in the

European rhetorical tradition, and to both Jonathan Rée and Barry Taylor for their insightful and generous criticisms.

Marilyn Malin was my agent at the time this book was first published. She was far more tolerant of the wayward course that I followed over the years than one has a right to expect from an agent. Although we have parted ways, I remain enormously grateful for her sharp intelligence and her support. I am grateful too to all those at Kingston University Press a decade ago, whose input and editorial guidance was so valuable, in particular to Siobhan Campbell .

It would be impossible to credit individually the many storytellers who have contributed to my love and appreciation of stories. Pascale Konyn first introduced me to the flourishing oral storytelling culture of the North-East of England, and I am grateful to the countless storytellers who performed in the candlelit murkiness of the Cumberland Arms, Newcastle.

In Maluku, Indonesia, a great many philosophers, storytellers and friends shared their tales, their understanding and their homes with me. In particular, I'd like to thank Matias Fatruan, Ibu Neli Batmomolin, Andrea Flew, Paay and Tin Suripatty and Benny Fenyapwain.

Over the years, since the publication of the first edition, I have had a small but enthusiastic band of readers who have found the book useful, interesting or diverting. It is for this reason that I have decided to re-release an updated version, rather than allowing the text to languish out-of-print. I am grateful to everyone who has read and given feedback on the book over the past decade.

In the acknowledgements to the first edition, I wrote about my sincere gratitude to friends and family, a gratitude I feel even more strongly now. Back then, I wrote of how my parents occasionally looked on in alarm as I have tried to find my own sea-legs. Hopefully, they are now more used to my haphazard voyages. Either way, they must take some of the credit for the fact that things have not turned out so badly after all. First time around, I dedicated this book to them, and the dedication still stands.

'*Tell me a story...*' Over fifteen years of friendship, Elee Kirk asked this of me many times, and she also shared a great many stories of her own. I cannot overstate her influence on the shape that this book has taken. She is very sorely missed.

The revised edition of the text was prepared while on a writing residency at the Parami Institute of the Liberal Arts and Sciences in Yangon, Myanmar. I am grateful to friends and colleagues in Yangon who made us feel so welcome in the city. Stan Jagger proofed the final manuscript, uncomplainingly braving the high seas of philosophy. Thanks are also due to my collaborator at Wind&Bones, Hannah Stevens, for all the new stories and new voyages we have launched together over the past few years.

If most of the work preparing this new edition was undertaken in Yangon, the finishing touches were made in Thessaloniki, within sight of Mount Olympus. No sane writer would fail to acknowledge the part played by local gods, spirits and *nats* in undertaking any enterprise. So I am grateful to all those deities who have been kindly enough not to throw too many spanners into the works.

NOTES

1. In the Marketplace in Darjeeling, Early One Morning

1. See, for example, the text quoted by Zimmer: 'The ocean of tears shed by each being, wandering through life after life, without beginning... is vaster than the Four Oceans together' (Zimmer 1969, 513).
2. The famous quote comes from Kierkegaard's *Purity of Heart is to Will One Thing* (Kierkegaard 1948, 102).
3. The text is the Hua-yen Sutra. See Liu (2006).
4. The censures against selling one's hair and 'wanton self-abuse' appear in Kant's *The Metaphysical Principles of Virtue*. The question of telling lies is dealt with in his *On a Supposed Right to Lie Because of Philanthropic Concerns*. For both sources, see Kant (1995).
5. This is the precise situation that Kant conjures up. In discussing this scenario, his defence of principle over everything else is curiously weak. If you told a lie, he says, then the would-be murderer might leave the house just as his intended victim, unbeknownst to you yourself, was heading out of the back door. Then they might meet and the murder might be committed. But if you told the truth, then as the thug was searching your house, the neighbours might come running and apprehend him. The moral of this tale is simple: if pursued by violent assailants, do not take refuge in the houses of Kantians.

2. All at Sea: A Philosophical Parable

1. Hegel identified Descartes as one such prophet, writing in his *Lectures on the History of Philosophy* that, with the arrival of Descartes on the philosophical scene, 'Here, we may say, we are at home, and like the mariner after a long voyage in a tempestuous sea, we may now hail the sight of land...' (Hegel 1995, 271).
2. In Plato's image of the cave, the philosophers return from the sunlight to tell those who are in the darkness about what they are missing. The idea of return as an essential part of wisdom also appears beyond the Western philosophical tradition. See, for example, the essays in Nagao (1991).
3. The passage from Aristophanes reads as follows:
   STUDENT: Chaerephon of Sphettus once asked Socrates whether

he was of the opinion that gnats produced their hum by way of the mouth or the rear end.

STREPSIADES: So what was his opinion about the gnat?

STUDENT: 'The intestinal passage of the gnat,' he said, 'is very narrow, and consequently the wind is forced to go straight through to the rear end. And then the arsehole, being an orifice forming the exit from this narrow passage, makes a noise owing to the force of this wind.'

STREPSIADES: So a gnat's arsehole is like a trumpet. How gutterly marvellous! I can see that defending a lawsuit successfully is going to be dead easy for someone who has such precise knowledge of the guts of gnats. (Aristophanes 2002, 80)

4. There is a distinction here between the idea that stories are like the sea, and the idea that storytelling and poetic activity are like sea-passages. The former image tends to blur the boundaries of individual stories, suggesting that stories live in continually shifting community with each other; the latter tends to preserve a kind of Aristotelian orderliness of stories as having—like a sea-passage from shore to shore—a beginning, a middle and an end.

3. Casting Off

1. The Kikori and Fly are two rivers in Southern Papua New Guinea, from where this story comes. The present retelling is an adaptation from the version by that wonderful storyteller, Geraldine McCaughrean (2001).

2. The passage from Sterne goes like this: 'To sum up all; there are archives at every stage to be look'd into, and rolls, records, documents, and endless genealogies, which justice ever and anon calls him back to stay the reading of: —In short, there is no end of it...' (Sterne 2003, 37).

A more contemporary version of the same thought appears in Patrick Neate's wonderful novel *Twelve Bar Blues*: 'Last thing I tell you is that stories don't have no beginning, middle an' end. That jus' a dumb-ass fantasy told by teachers to school' (Neate 2002, 248).

This, of course was also Scheherazade's ruse, that cunning woman who left her stories forever unfinished and so saved her own life.

3. Once again, I am indebted to McCaughrean (2001) for her version of this Roma tale. My own version is a rather free retelling of McCaughrean's.

4. The passage from Bernard's *Apologia* reads as follows, and could be seen as a diatribe not only against art, but also against the kind of imaginative extravagance and mixing that goes on in storytelling and representation in general:

'And further, in the cloisters, under the eyes of the brethren engaged in reading, what business has there that ridiculous monstrosity, that amazing misshapen shapeliness and shapely misshapenness. Those unclean monkeys? Those fierce lions? Those monstrous centaurs? Those semi-human beings? Those spotted tigers? Those fighting warriors? Those huntsmen blowing their horns? Here you behold several bodies beneath one head; there again several heads upon one body. Here you see a quadruped with the tail of a serpent; there a fish with the head of a quadruped. There an animal suggests a horse in front and half a goat behind; here a horned beast exhibits the rear parts of a horse. In fine, on all sides there appears so rich and so amazing a variety of forms that it is more delightful to read the marbles than the manuscripts, and to spend the whole day in admiring these things, piece by piece, rather than in meditating the Law Divine.' (Barasch 2000, 96)

5. At the same time, storytelling has a remarkable mnemonic value, as demonstrated by Elizabeth and Paul Barber's fascinating book *When they Severed Earth from Sky*, which explores the suggestion that some of the most ancient of our myths may, in fact, encode remarkably precise knowledge about human history and pre-history (Barber and Barber, 2006). The art of storytelling is, of course, related to the art of memory. And perhaps both are in turn related to the art of wisdom. But storytelling is not reducible to the information that the story may encode mnemonically.

6. Kierkegaard is writing about the story of Abraham and Isaac. Anyone who saw Abraham's raising of the knife would be paralysed, he says, and anybody who saw Abraham's unclouded determination would be blinded. 'And yet rare enough though they may be, those who are both paralysed and blind, still more rare is he who can tell the story and give it its due' (Kierkegaard 1985, 55).

7. Western philosophy, it appears, is not entirely woodpecker-free. Woodpeckers are discussed in Aristotle's *History of Animals*, where they are said to have broad, flat tongues, and where the philosopher reflects upon their ability to detect vibrations beneath the bark of trees (Nussbaum 1992, 236-7). Woodpeckers also make an appearance in William James's *Pragmatism* while he is discussing theories of design in nature (James 1980), and in an essay by Carnap (Carnap 1995, 261). Robert Audi reflects upon his knowledge of woodpeckers from the sound of their tapping in his book on epistemology (Audi 1998, 150), and Heidegger speculates on the fact that what we hear when hiking heartily through the Black Forest is not 'pure sound' but always the creak of a wagon or the tapping of a woodpecker (Heidegger 1978, 207). In India, although there seem to be relatively few strictly philosophical woodpeckers, the birds do nevertheless make an appearance in Aryasura's *Jatakamala* (Khoroche and Doniger, 1989). In Chinese texts, on the other hand, they seem decidedly rare: far rarer, indeed, than even phoenixes.

8. Michel Serres writes that, 'When languages talk about themselves, they begin the circle again. They come from rumour in a whirlwind. First

through echo, repetition. Then through redundancy. Then through rhythm and cadence. These circles follow one another every which way' (Serres 1995, 70). Despite this impossibility of standing outside, knowledge, understanding and philosophy are all still possible. It may be that the circles are not vicious, except from the point of view of one who still dreams of dry land.

4. Storytelling and Experience

1. It may be worth mentioning here why I have chosen to speak of 'stories' rather than the more familiar 'narrative'. There is today an enormous amount of interest in storytelling in a wide range of diverse fields: from philosophy to cognitive science to religious studies—a small handful of examples might include Niles (1999), Bruner (2003), O'Flaherty (1990), MacIntyre (1997), Turner (1997) and Dennett (1992). Given the sheer profusion of work that aims to explore the relevance of stories for diverse areas of human knowledge, the precise understanding of what constitutes a narrative or a story differs considerably from text to text.

   My own preference for the term 'story' over the term 'narrative' is rooted in the suspicion that 'narrative' sounds unnecessarily clinical. Nobody says to another human being, 'Go on, tell me a narrative!'; and as what interests me here is not just the story as a *bearer of content*, but also the *act of telling*, 'story' suits my needs better. What philosophers and literary critics study as 'narrative' is often the corpse of a story laid out on the table for literary or philosophical dissection. Such analysis may be useful, but just as we cannot understand what it is to be human merely on the basis of information gleaned from autopsies, so we cannot understand what is at stake in the telling of a story merely through looking at the story divested of all the liveliness of the telling.

2. Here I cannot resist a digression on the experience of pilots. Once, in the tiny airport outside Saumlaki in the Tanimbar islands, Indonesia, I was waiting for a small ten-seater plane to take me back to the regional capital: the only flight for two weeks. The weather was terrible, the palm-trees on the far side of the airstrip were almost bent double, and the clouds were rumbling with thunder. It was only a small plane. I went to speak to a friend who worked in the airport. 'This weather is awful,' I said. 'Do you think the flight might be cancelled?' My friend smiled calmly. 'Don't worry,' she reassured me. 'You'll catch your flight. The pilot is very brave...'

3. In an earlier essay, 'The Crisis of the Novel,' Benjamin rehearses the ancient tropes of narrative as a sea, writing that 'From the point of view of epic, existence is an ocean. Nothing is more epic than the sea' (Benjamin 1999, 299). However, land-lubber that he is, he claims that the

writer of the epic is simply one who lounges on the beach and *contemplates* the ocean. The novelist, on the other hand, sets off on the waves, as Horace and Virgil set out. Benjamin seems to fear such lonely journeys. This is perhaps one of the less convincing aspects of Benjamin's essay: his determination to drive a wedge between oral and written forms of storytelling, and his assertion that while the storyteller draws from experience, the novelist draws from isolation and thus 'lacks counsel and can give none' (Benjamin 2006, 146). This is a claim that may be justifiably contested as unduly harsh by both novelists and their readers, although Benjamin's reasons for making this distinction are less to do with a misplaced Romanticism and more to do with his concern with material, historical conditions: if we live in an age in which the work of the hand has declined, this will inevitably have an effect on the way we relate to (and relate!) our tales. Yet the novel is often a more mixed and sociable literary form than Benjamin allows: less a lonely skiff adrift in a sea of solitude, and more a clamorous community with its multitudes of sailors and prophets and disputing voices, one that does not stand apart from the liquid tapestry of human experience. See Jay (1998) for one attempt to cast the novel in a rather better light without taking leave of Benjamin's thought entirely.

4. Intriguingly, the notion that there may be a connection between the work of the hand and storytelling is one that has been given a renewed impetus by recent—albeit speculative—theories of the origins of language that consider language as originally gestural, and that see *speech* as a development of an originally gestural language that frees up the hands for precisely the kind of work about which Benjamin writes. Although this is an idea that goes back to Condillac in the eighteenth century, it has recently been revived amongst scholars concerned with the origins of language. See Gentilucci and Corballis (2007) for a good overview.

5. Rosenzweig's argument, although addressed at the philosophical tradition in general, is directed more specifically at Hegel, for whom the self-superseding itinerary of *Geist*—mind or spirit—from simple sense consciousness to absolute knowing, ends in a knowledge that is independent of time. Hegel writes:

'Time is the Notion itself that is there and which presents itself to consciousness as empty intuition; for this reason, Spirit (*Geist*) necessarily appears in Time, and it appears in Time just so long as it has not grasped its pure Notion, i.e. has not annulled Time. It is the outer, intuited pure Self which is not grasped by the Self, the merely intuited Notion; when this latter grasps itself it sets aside its Time-form, comprehends this intuiting, and is a comprehended and comprehending intuiting. Time, therefore, appears as the destiny and necessity of Spirit that is not yet complete within itself...' (Hegel 1979, 487)

Hegel's Absolute knowing stands outside—or, rather, it *sets aside*—the temporal form that has led to this very knowledge. This setting aside of time is, Rosenzweig maintains, deceitful.

6. Storytelling is not the only method advanced by Rosenzweig, although it is the one that interests me here. Instead, he suggests that there could be a threefold method, consisting of storytelling, face-to-face conversation and 'communal singing'. Rosenzweig's concern with storytelling stems from his reading of Schelling, who also attempted to construct a narrative philosophy in his *Ages of the World*. Schelling's work begins with the following line: 'The past is known, the present is recognised, The future is divined. What is known is recounted, what is recognised is presented, what is divined is prophesied.' (Translation by Judith Norman, in Žižek (1997, 113)).

 Here it is possible to see the rationale for what seems, initially at least, to be a rather curious list of philosophical methods, storytelling, conversation and communal singing all being methods that strongly correlate with Schelling's triad of recounting (storytelling), presenting (making-present, speaking to those who are present) and prophecy (the ritualistic singing of shared hopes for the future and of things to come).

7. Rosenzweig's thinking is profoundly entangled with theological and religious concerns. I am deliberately leaving these concerns upon one side (as I will also do in the later sections of this book with the work of Levinas). In part, this is because I am interested far more in the nature of experience than in the baffling thicket of difficulties that is theology: whenever philosophers talk about God, I confess that I have not the slightest idea what they might be talking about. My mind, alas, is simply not dei-form (McGhee 2000, 123), and I can make no sense of this kind of language. As a result, my reading of Rosenzweig is robustly non-religious. If I were pressed to justify this, I would do so by saying that it is a decision that could be seen to be sanctioned by Rosenzweig himself when he makes the claim that his work, despite all appearances to the contrary, is not concerned with the philosophy of religion (Rosenzweig 1998, 69).

8. How often, Rosenzweig asks, have utopian dreams of dry land and of absolute moral certainty led to slaughter and destruction? (Rosenzweig 1985, 271)

9. In his well-judged essay 'Against Narrative', Galen Strawson attacks the 'fashionable' obsession with narrative as a means to self-understanding. Strawson contrasts those who are 'diachronic' in their self-understanding, and those who are 'episodic', putting himself in the latter camp. I, like Strawson, tend more towards the episodic than the diachronic, which is to say that I am in considerable sympathy when Strawson writes 'I have absolutely no sense of my life as a narrative with form, or indeed as a narrative without form. Absolutely none'

(Strawson 2004, 433). But whilst I agree with Strawson that the idea of the self as a story is both limiting and mistaken, and with his defence of 'Episodic' experience, when we allow for the multiplicity and fluidity that Rushdie highlights and that is suggested by Benjamin and Rosenzweig, we can see that this claim that we are *Homo narrans* simply implies that we are creatures who cannot but spin tales, but does not imply either that these tales are single or that they are necessarily concerned with self-understanding or identity. Indeed, it may be that that freeing the concern with narrative from the concern with identity opens the door to a broader understanding of what story-thinking is.

10. Mendes-Flohr (2006, 47) draws more explicit connections between Rosenzweig's work and the phenomenological theories current in Germany at the time that Rosenzweig was writing.

11. Caution is, of course, often seen as being something close to the paradigmatic philosophical virtue. However, any navigator will tell you that while caution may be useful when it is judiciously employed, excessive caution is at least as risky as excessive foolhardiness.

12. This, of course, comes from the ancient Greeks. Heraclitus said that one could not step into the same river twice; Cratylus retorted that one could not step into the same river once. The Indian philosopher Nagarjuna, on the other hand, might trump Cratylus's card by contending that there is nobody to step, whether into a river or anywhere else, nor is there anything to step into, nor, for that matter, is there any stepping to be done: 'Neither an entity nor a nonentity / Moves in any of the three ways. / So motion, mover / and route are nonexistent.' (Garfield 1995, 133)

5. A Naïve Phenomenology of Ethics

1. If this imperative is experiential, then it is neither hypothetical ('If you are in situation A then you should do B') *nor* is it categorical ('In all circumstances, you should act according to C'). Instead, it is a third kind of imperative, one that takes its force from the particularity of the situation—and thus that cannot be categorical in the sense that Kantian philosophers use the term—but that is nevertheless anything but hypothetical.

2. There are some interesting perspectives on the failure of Husserl's project in the work of Ströker (1997) and Kolakowski (1987).

3. The passage from Aristotle appears in *Metaphysics* 982 b18.

4. As an officer, Levinas was spared deportation to the concentration camps. His family back home in Lithuania were not so lucky, and were murdered by the Nazis. Meanwhile his wife and daughter were hidden,

with the help of the philosopher Maurice Blanchot, in a monastery in Orléans.

5. Here it can already be seen how Levinas can resolve the apparent paradox of using the methods of Husserl to address Rosenzweig's concerns. If the other person is inaccessible to me, then here in my encounter with another person there is already a limit to the totalising dreams of philosophy, to Rosenzweig's 'cognition of the All'.

6. The difficulty of pinning down with absolute precision what Levinas means by the 'face' is one that has exercised a great many of Levinas's critics, and even his supporters. But I'm not sure that when it comes to the face we are dealing with something that is capable of that kind of philosophical precision. Perhaps the closest Levinas himself comes to a definition is in his book *God, Death and Time*, where he writes, 'That which Descartes makes a substance, all the while protesting against the image of the pilot in his vessel, that from which Leibniz makes a monad, that which Plato posits as the soul contemplating the Ideas, that which Spinoza thinks as a mode of thought, is described phenomenologically as a face. Without this phenomenology, one is pushed toward a reification of the soul, whereas here a problem other than to be or not to be is posed, a problem prior to that question' (Levinas 2001b, 12).

7. I discuss the ambivalences of Levinas as a storyteller at much greater length in my book *Levinas, Storytelling and Anti-Storytelling* (Buckingham 2013).

8. Regarding *Totality and Infinity*, Derrida points out in a footnote to his essay 'Violence and Metaphysics' that 'it seems to us impossible, essentially impossible, that it could have been written by a woman. Its philosophical subject is man (*vir*)' (Derrida 1987, 321).

The gendered nature of the stories that Levinas tells, and the implications of this gendering, have been explored extensively by a number of writers including Chanter (2002), Katz (2004), Sandford (2000) and Irigaray (1986).

This overbearingly patriarchal mood continues when Levinas turns at the end of *Totality and Infinity* to explore the subject of community in an attempt to answer the question, 'Why am I bound to society at all?' (Gibbs 1994, 28). The argument Levinas makes is too complex to explore in detail here, but it begins with a consideration of the relationship of paternity (note the patriarchal slant, once again), the relationship I have with the child, a relationship with that which is 'my own and non-mine, a possibility of myself but also a possibility of the other' (Levinas 1969, 267). Levinas is not necessarily talking about actual paternity here: he may also be talking about the way that, in reading Levinas (for example), something is engendered in me, and the possibilities of Levinas become my possibilities. This is the kind of engendering that leads Douglas Hofstadter, in his book *I am a Strange Loop* to talk about the interpenetration of 'souls' (Hofstadter, 2008); and it leads Levinas to move from the idea of shared paternity to the idea of fraternity (see Llewelyn (1995, 137) —once again, this is not necessarily biological fraternity: we could as well be talking about the 'fraternity' of Levinas readers), and from here to recognising the possibility of society conceived of on the model of brotherhood, as a 'collectivity that is not a communion' (Levinas 1987, 94). Despite some noble attempts to exonerate Levinas from accusations of patriarchal bias, for example in Katz (2004, 162), one still can't help thinking that this whole story—which is a matter of sons, fathers and brothers—is both troubling and profoundly lacking in the way that it has consigned daughters, mothers and sisters to silence.

9. For Levinas, this metaphysical quest is, in the end, something not separated from philosophy, the task of which is to testify to this possibility of ethics. Levinas shares this idea of philosophy as a form of metaphysical quest with William James: 'Metaphysics has usually followed a very primitive kind of quest. You know how men have always hankered after unlawful magic, and you know what a great part in magic words have always played. If you have his name, or the formula of incantation that binds him, you can control the spirit, genie, afrite, or whatever the power may be. Solomon knew the names of all the spirits, and having their names, he held them subject to his will. So the universe has always appeared to the natural mind as a kind of enigma, of which the key must be sought in the shape of some illuminating or power-bringing word or name. That word names the universe's principle, and to possess it is after a fashion to possess the universe itself. "God," "Matter," "Reason," "the Absolute," "Energy," are so many solving names. You can rest when you have them. You are at the end of your metaphysical quest.' (James 1980, 28) However, having said that the quest comes to an end in possession, he cautions that in his own pragmatic approach, the response to the initial problem 'appears less as a solution, then, than as a program for more work.'

I would add to this—and Levinas, I think, would be in broad agreement—that a metaphysical quest proper is one in which there is no solution: the purpose of the metaphysical quest is to lead us onwards, and not to reach some kind of terminus.

10. In talking of this interweaving, MacDonald draws connections between Levinas's thinking and that of Hegel, and while both of them share a tendency to move between narrative and argument, as John Llewelyn points out, the dénouements of the dramas in Levinas's *Totality and Infinity* and Hegel's *Phenomenology of Spirit* are very different (Llewelyn 1995, 27). For Hegel, the end-point is the annulment of time itself, and the stages of the journey are 'less historical moments of history than logical moments of an Absolute Idea that transcends the chronic time of historical narrative' (MacDonald 2005, 182); for Levinas, on the other hand,

there is an attempt to present a drama that has no end point, but that consists of a complex set of forces that pull in different directions and that, in doing so, open up the possibility of goodness in the heart of the tragedy that he is weaving.

11. It is perhaps for this reason that in his later work, *Otherwise than Being*, Levinas explicitly sets out to leave stories behind and to move beyond a 'narrative, epic, way of speaking' (Levinas 1981, 13). In doing so he comes perilously close to confessing the story-like structure of the earlier book; but he also lends the later book a curiously non-linear texture that, although it no longer has any clear threads of narrative, has lost none of the high drama of his earlier work, being riven throughout with an astonishingly heightened language of which the following is only an example: 'Vulnerability, exposure to outrage, to wounding, passivity more passive than all patience, passivity of the accusative form, trauma of accusation suffered by a hostage to the point of persecution, implicating the identity of the hostage who substitutes himself for the others: all this is the self, a defecting or defeat of the ego's identity.' (Levinas 1981, 15)

Simon Critchley writes of Levinas's prose style in his later book as arising out of a commitment 'like Plato, to an anti-rhetorical rhetoric, a writing against writing' (Critchley 1996, 115). One might add—given that the language of outrage, exposure and wounding seems like an irresistible temptation to tell stories—that this also looks like a kind of storytelling against storytelling. See my book *Levinas, Storytelling and Anti-Storytelling* (Buckingham 2013).

12. Levinas writes that 'the exceptional structure of aesthetic existence invokes this singular term magic, which will enable us to make the somewhat worn-out notion of passivity precise and concrete' (Levinas 1998a, 3).

13. Michel Camille's fascinating book (Camille 1991) explores the role of the idol in Western thought in considerable depth.

14. In actual fact, Levinas's dismissal of storytelling is not outright. Under the influence of Maurice Blanchot—see, for example, Blanchot (1996, 381)—he notes that poetic language may also allow us to recognise the very ambiguity of language, the fact that—in a strikingly liquid metaphor—'Each word-meaning is at the confluence of innumerable semantic rivers' (Levinas 1998a, 77). Poetic speech may not do the job of prose, but poetry—and at one point Levinas suggests only poetry (Levinas 2001, 51)—can still return us not only to the fact that language is not only always equivocal, but also to the fact that it has to it a kind of materiality. Words, in other words, are things too (Blanchot 1996, 383), and representation is never a straightforwardly mimetic process. Not only this, but words, in their brute material nature, can break with the rhythm of incantation, can make us stumble, can bring us up short. And here

Levinas sees that literature can have a role, both in challenging our belief in straightforward representation and in breaking with, rather than in weaving, the enchantments of language.

15. Alford's article, significantly, leaves the answer to this question open.

16. Perhaps it is to this fact that Levinas is referring when he points out how the *characters* within a play leave no traces upon the stage (Levinas 2001, 14).

17. Note, too, that Bachelard's 'gentle mania' is the very same mania diagnosed by Rosenzweig: the habit of always positing that a subject must accompany any possible experience. If Bachelard gets away with this, it is precisely because of his ironic distance, and the gentleness by virtue of which he recognises that this *is*, after all, a form of mania.

18. Nor, it should also be added, is it *ethically* more correct.

6. Stories About Stories

1. Such stories, as will become apparent, are by no means uncommon: it is not merely within that particular form of literature referred to, whether admiringly or dismissively, as 'postmodern' that stories can be seen to question their own telling or their own nature as stories.

2. The technical term for this nesting of stories is 'recursion'. Many of the stories that I am exploring here exhibit forms of recursion—and some of the Indian tales and collections of tales I am drawing on show what happens when recursion runs riot. As recursion seems to be, in one fashion or another, central to so many of our stories, one might be tempted to think that such recursion in one form or another is fundamental not just to human storytelling, but to human thought. But we need to be cautious. In his fascinating account of life and thought amongst the Pirahã in the Amazon basin, *Don't Sleep, There are Snakes* (Everett, 2008), Daniel Everett makes the astonishing claim that the Pirahã simply have no recursion as we would understand it. Everett provides some fascinating examples of Pirahã stories that demonstrate what storytelling without recursion looks like.

3. Derrida does not agree, claiming that there is a moral of the story, but that this moral is 'morality itself' (Derrida 1996, 66). He goes on to explain that in the story we encounter the everyday fact that in my responding to the call of duty or to the obligations upon me, there is also a necessary ethical betrayal: 'I cannot respond to the call, the request, the obligation, or even the love of another without sacrificing the other other, the other others' (Derrida 1996, 68). Of course, it is possible to derive this proposition from the story, but in doing so I fear that we risk losing the shudder of thought of which Kierkegaard writes.

4. See Varela (1993) and Lakoff and Johnson (1999). One can try an inter-

esting experiment here. Find a quiet place, free of distraction, and sit down with your eyes closed. Now pay attention to the arising of thoughts, and ask yourself if you can track a single thought that you can be certain takes place unaccompanied by subtle changes in bodily sensation, or movements within the body—perhaps by changes in the rhythm of the breath, by movements of the eye muscles, or by a tightening of the muscles of the belly.

5. Serres himself makes a similar point in *Genesis* (Serres 1995, 138). William Paulson, in 'Swimming the Channel', his study of Serres, language and translation, notes that 'Serres is a philosopher arguing that stories are more fundamental than arguments, a writer telling the story that in the beginning was not the word' (Paulson 2005, 35).

6. Walter Ong explores these questions in considerable depth in his book *Orality and Literacy* (Ong 2002).

7. See Ong (2002) for more about the technologies of writing and the decline of the art of memory.

8. This may strike the followers of Derrida as impossibly naïve. But here I want to put aside the arguments for and against logocentrism (which may turn out in the end not to be the most interesting arguments), and to give primacy instead to the body, to the flesh-and-blood embodiment of a person who is exposed in the telling of a story.

9. We can take 'the same story' here as a phenomenological given. We hear a story, and we read it, and we say, 'yes, this is the same story'. Similarly, when Kierkegaard embarks upon his four retellings, we recognise that these are the 'same' as the story in Genesis. As tellings diverge, of course, there is no point at which we can say for certain that they are the same story or different stories. We do not have to be caught between the two poles of absolute identity and absolute difference. 'Same' and 'different' in this context are fuzzy, imprecise, everyday judgements, not judgements rooted in firmly grounded philosophical certainties.

10. If we have forgotten the embodiment of language in both speech and in writing, if language has become somehow abstract, perhaps it is not so much because of the fact of writing itself as it is on account of the growth of silent reading, which mutes—but does not remove—the embodiment of language. Silent reading appears relatively late in the traditions of the West. The first clear reference is in Augustine's *Confessions*, where Augustine notes with astonishment that Ambrose read with his eyes scanning the page and his tongue held still, but this, at the time, was a novelty. By the tenth century, Manguel (1996) claims silent reading was becoming more commonplace, but even as late as the nineteenth century, it was common to share a book through reading aloud rather than to read in silence. Nevertheless, for all our silent reading, this silence is only under certain conditions. Language itself has not become silent. The marketplace is not still and hushed. We remain garrulous. And if the shudder of

thought is muted in our seclusion, in our silent reading and writing, it is there all the same.

11. Ricoeur himself deals with this gap by taking a different path from the one taken here. He agrees that stories are indeed lived, but says that they are lived 'in the mode of the imaginary' (Ricoeur 1991, 26). At the same time, he maintains that life itself cannot be understood outside of our capacity to narrate: 'fiction, in particular narrative fiction, is an irreducible dimension of self-understanding' (Ricoeur 1991, 30). The claim being made here, however, is a stronger claim than that made by Ricoeur: for if we take seriously Kierkegaard's shudder, then we can see that stories are not merely lived in the mode of the imaginary, but they are also lived in the flesh; and we can also see that if we do not make such a radical distinction between stories and life at the outset, then we are spared the labour of having to stitch them back together with Ricoeur's painstaking care.

12. The actual origin of this tale is somewhat tricky to pin down. Ahir cites it as number 499 (Ahir 2000, 24) in the enormous body of canonical Jataka tales, although Cowell's translation of Jataka 499, despite having Sivi as the main character, features neither hawks nor doves (Cowell 1990, 250-6). The story appears in art in the Ajanta caves, and turns up in the *Mahabharata*. It also occurs in Somadeva's twelfth century compilation of stories the *Kathasaritsagara* (Somadeva 1996, 45), and is discussed in the Siksha Samuccaya, a compilation by the eighth-century philosopher Shantideva (Bendall & Rouse 2000, 99). It has reappeared more recently in a retelling by R. K. Narayan, in his book Gods, *Demons and Others* (Narayan 1994). My own retelling adds yet another non-canonical version to the many non-canonical versions that exist. As the story does not appear in the canonical set of Jatakas, it seems that there is no canonical version, merely a proliferation of non-canonical versions.

13. The Buddhist tradition from which this story comes was fully aware of these two possibilities, dividing texts into those that are to be read literally (*nitartha*) and those that are to be interpreted (*neyartha*) (Lamotte 1993, 16).

14. Not long ago, I was discussing the Jataka literature with an eminent scholar-monk from Myanmar. He was insistent that these stories were distinguished from all others by virtue of being *true*, not in an allegorical sense, but in a literal sense.

15. Kierkegaard writes of the story of Abraham and Isaac that anyone who saw Abraham's raising of the knife would be paralysed, and anybody who saw Abraham's unclouded determination would be blinded. Then he writes, 'And yet rare enough though they may be, those who are both paralysed and blind, still more rare is he who can tell the story and give it its due' (Kierkegaard 1985, 55).

16. At this point, it may be protested that this is mere invention, that I have

made up this story to suit my purposes, and so this shuddering itself never happened. I could equally well have had the villagers returning home unaffected by the story. This is no doubt true. But it is enough merely to suggest that the story of King Sivi is capable of having such an effect, that even as philosophers, we do not encounter stories primarily as the bearers of philosophical understanding, but on the contrary we encounter them as living, breathing creatures capable of shuddering. Any reading that attempts to explain the story must also pay attention to at least the possibility of this shudder.

17. Assad makes a similar point in relation to Serres's own approach, claiming that in his practice of philosophy Serres often does away with the very 'analytical methods' that are themselves considered as essential to philosophy (Assad 1999, 164).

7. Stories about Time

1. Ramanujan goes on to claim that this is an indication of a kind of materialism in Indian thought. 'Thus, all things, even so-called non-material ones like space and time or caste, affect other things because all things are "substantial" (*dhatu*). The only difference is that some are subtle (*sushkma*), some gross (*sthula*). Contrary to the notion that Indians are "spiritual", they are really "material minded". They are materialists, believers in substance...' (Ramanujan 1998, 46).

2. The curious history of the Indian Rope Trick—a trick that was often imagined but never performed—is entertainingly told by the historian Peter Lamont in his book, *The Rise of the Indian Rope Trick* (Lamont 2005). The inclusion of the rope trick here is an anachronism, given that, as Lamont points out, the trick was a recent—and wholly imaginary —invention.

3. The magical art of making blocks of wood appear to be elephants—a neat trick if you can pull it off—is one that greatly preoccupied metaphysicians from the Yogacara tradition of Buddhism. See Garfield (2001, 133-4).

4. In the original context, the temporal complexity of the story is even more elaborate on account of the multiple framings of the text discussed above.

5. Or, as Conor Oberst sings, 'How time can move / both fast and slow / amazes me.'

6. Here, when talking about time, I am talking about time as experienced: I am certainly not talking about the kinds of questions that the physicists talk about when they talk about time. Questions as deep as these should be left, I believe, to those who can do the maths—and, alas, am not included amongst their number.

7. The version of the tale told here comes from McKinnon (1992) and from Karel Mouw's translation of Petrus Drabbe's ethnography of the Tanimbar Islands *Het Leven Van Den Tanembarees*, translated into Indonesian as *Ethnografi Tanimbar*. The story as it is told here, and the reading of the story that is given, owe a debt to several Tanimbarese philosophers, in particular sculptor Matias Fatruan of Sera.

8. I have explored these stories at much greater length in my book *Stealing With the Eyes: Imaginings and Incantations in Indonesia* (Haus Publishing, 2018).

9. Of course, this is only true at the beginning of the story. Indeed, it is possible to detect in Tanimbarese conceptions of time a distinct drift away from seeing time in terms of locality, towards the idea of time as universal. Matias Fatruan, one of the most perceptive commentators on time in the Tanimbar islands, divided time into three eras: the *jaman purba* or ancient age, the time before Atuf speared the sun; the *jaman pertengahan*, the 'middle ages' of traditional Tanimbarese culture, before the coming of the Catholic missionaries in 1912; and the *jaman moderen*, the modern era from 1912 onwards. While the *jaman purba* and *jaman pertengahan* are seen as local times ('Things were different here,' my Tanimbarese philosopher friends used to say), the *jaman moderen* is seen as a global time.

   As in Europe where time became less local and more global with the coming of the railways, so with the arrival of timetables—whether the liturgical timetables of the church year, or the timetables used in schools, offices, or for public transport—time has come to be seen in Tanimbar as taking on an increasingly universal character. However, in myths such as the myth of Atuf, it could be said that the Tanimbarese go further than Kant, for Kant is still caught up by what Deleuze and Guattari (2001, 18) call the 'specifically European disease' of transcendence.

10. In traditional Buddhist cosmology, for example, gods are long-lived but ultimately mortal.

11. See McKinnon (1992).

12. The Buddhists, for example, satirise the idea of a creator god by parodying Brahma, the creator in the Indian pantheon, as a god who is driven by loneliness to the delusion that is a creator, whereas he is—as we all are—in fact a creation of the world. See Gombrich (1996, 81).

8. Stories about Others

1. 'L'absolutement Autre, c'est Autrui.' Where Husserl in his *Cartesian Meditations* uses the terms 'the other person,' or 'someone else', Levinas prefers the more portentous 'Other', in an attempt to give a sense that we

are not talking about the other person as a thing in the world, but precisely as a *person* who is, for that reason, inaccessible to us.

2. The idea of multiple drafts comes from Dan Dennett's *Consciousness Explained* (Dennett 1992). There is a burgeoning body of experimental evidence that increasingly demonstrates the unreliability of our first-person reports about what is actually going on in our consciousness. Some examples include the work on change blindness by Simons (2000), on inattentional blindness by Simons and Chabris (1999) and Mack et al. (1998), on the timing of consciousness by Libet (2004), and on the experience of free-will by Wegner (2002). Literature such as this should give any armchair phenomenologist reason to feel just a little bit queasy.

3. Even though we have already seen that King Sivi found himself infinitely responsible for a bird. Dermot Moran, in his introduction to phenomenology, asks this very question of Levinas, writing that Levinas's inability to satisfactorily answer this question is 'an extraordinarily serious admission'. If, Moran writes, Levinas cannot provide a criterion of 'facehood', then it is not clear that he is giving a philosophy of the face at all (Moran 1999, 350).

4. Not, at least as we understand it. The question of whether fish sleep is, in fact, an arid one and depends entirely upon what one's definition of sleep is. Fish certainly rest, although having no eyelids, they don't close their eyes. In a state of rest, it seems that a fish has only slightly impaired awareness, very different from the temporary suspension of awareness in mammals.

5. There are Buddhist cases of wrong-doers being reborn as fish as well, for example in the decidedly unpleasant commentarial story to verses 334-337 of the *Dhammapada*. Here Kapila the monk, having taught several doctrinally suspect positions, is reborn in hell for generations (a fate that might be enough to make anyone shy away from teaching anything whatsoever), and after aeons of suffering in hell, he is eventually reborn once again as a fish with a beautiful golden body, but with extremely bad breath. On being caught, the fish is taken to the Buddha who explains that the fish has such a terrible smell on account of his previous bad deeds. Then the fish dies and, once more, is reborn in hell. Rebirth as a fish is not always bad, however—even if rebirth as a fish with halitosis perhaps is—as the Jataka tales of the Buddha's previous incarnations, some of them in fishy form, demonstrate.

6. In this, then, the fish is different from the poor cave-dweller in Plato's *Republic*. One who sits in the cave before the flickering shadows at least has the chance of hearing the truths spoken by a philosopher who has made it to the surface; but apparently, no such possibility exists in the world of fish.

7. Spelling adapted to reflect pinyin Romanisation.

8. The translation that Heidegger used was that by Martin Buber, the first

translation of the *Zhuangzi* into German, published in 1910. See May (1996, 4).

9. Zhuangzi's claim that the fish are having fun might be considered to be an abject example of anthropomorphism. However, if we refuse to see the animal kingdom as a kingdom of Cartesian automatons and if we admit that we ourselves are continuous with animal others, then there is no reason to rule out of court too readily the possibility that certain simple—or even more complex—pleasures, are not exclusively human. If perhaps fish do sleep, then perhaps fish do have fun: only their fun and their sleep are different to ours. This argument is pursued with some vigour in the book by Balcombe (2007).

10. Here, the error may lie in our imaginations. At an exhibition at the Cité des Sciences in Paris in 2007, I came across a disconcerting recording of a shoal of fish screaming in apparent panic.

11. 'Talking Fish Stuns New York', BBC News Online, 16th March 2003: http://news.bbc.co.uk/2/hi/americas/2854189.stm

12. An *ikat* is kind of woven fabric. 'Ikat' literally means 'knot'.

13. One wonders what Levinas would have made of a fish who prophesied (and in Hebrew, at that). For Levinas, there is indeed a kind of prophecy in the relationship with the other, a prophecy in which 'the Infinite passes—and awakens' Levinas, (1996, 146-7); but when the passing Infinite takes on the form of a fish, then we are finding ourselves rather a long way from Levinas's thinking.

14. Chatwin goes on to discuss the paradox of the monotheistic faiths arising from 'within the ambit of the desert,' but then notes that 'the desert people themselves show an indifference towards the Almighty that is decidedly cavalier. "We will go up to God and salute him," said a bedu to Palgrave in the 1860s, "and if he proves hospitable, we will stay with him: if otherwise, we will mount our horses and ride off"' (Chatwin 1988, 199).

15. The parallel here with Heidegger's distinction between fear—the fear of this or that—and anxiety, which has no object, is clear. Heidegger writes that, 'Anxiety is basically different from fear. We become afraid in the face of this or that particular being that threatens us in this or that particular respect. Fear in the face of something is also in each case a fear for something in particular. Because fear possesses this trait of being "fear in the face of" and "fear for," he who fears and is afraid is captive to the mood in which he finds himself. Striving to rescue himself from this particular thing, he becomes unsure of everything else and completely "loses his head." Anxiety does not let such confusion arise. Much to the contrary, a peculiar calm pervades it. Anxiety is indeed anxiety in the face of ..., but not in the face of this or that thing. Anxiety in the face of ... is always anxiety for ..., but not for this or that' (Heidegger 1993, 100). However, while for Heidegger anxiety brings to light a kind of temporal

unity of our existence here in the world, for Levinas metaphysical desire leads to all kinds of fissures, to radical splits and disunities.

16. Levinas's move from the recognition of our restlessness to the idea of absolute otherness takes place in several stages. Firstly, he distinguishes between desire and need. Secondly, he distinguishes between that towards which desire is directed and that towards which need is directed, invoking his grail, the absolute otherness that is the face of the other person. Having invoked this object or pseudo-object that is not, he claims, a part of the order of things, Levinas can now make a final move by insisting that the face of the other has the dimension of height, being transcendent to all objects. We have arrived at transcendence, the good (and a curious idea of God) beyond being entirely. Levinas makes the point as follows, coining the term 'transascendence' to stress the upward dimension. 'The very dimension of height is opened up by metaphysical Desire. That this height is no longer the heavens but the Invisible is the very elevation of height and its nobility... the metaphysical movement is transcendent, and transcendence, like desire and inadequation, is necessarily a transascendence.' (Levinas 1969, 35)

  But the argument seems circular. The dimension of height is assumed at the outset in the very distinction between need and desire, only to be pulled like a rabbit from a hat in the final move.

17. 'If the world may be thought of as a certain definite quantity of force and as a certain definite number of centres of force—and every other representation remains indefinite and therefore useless—it follows that, in the great dice game of existence, it must pass through a calculable number of combinations. In infinite time, every possible combination would at some time or another be realised; more: it would be realised an infinite number of times. And since between every combination and its next recurrence all other possible combinations would have to take place, and each of these combinations conditions the entire sequence of combinations in the same series, a circular movement of absolutely identical series is thus demonstrated: the world as a circular movement that has already repeated itself infinitely often and plays its game in infinitum' (Nietzsche 1973, 549). The *Will to Power* makes clear that the doctrine of eternal recurrence is not merely a psychological device. Nietzsche is also making a metaphysical claim about how the universe necessarily must be. Regardless of the cogency of Nietzsche's argument, the point being argued here is unaffected.

Afterword to the Revised Edition

1. Here I am thinking, in particular, of François Jullien's work on blandness. See Jullien (2007).

BIBLIOGRAPHY

Ahir, D.C. *Influence of the Jatakas on Art and Literature*. New Delhi: B.R. Publishing, 2000.

Alford, C. Fred, "Levinas and Political Theory," *Political Theory* 32 no.2 (2004): 146—71.

Aristophanes, *Lysistrata and Other Plays: The Acharnians, The Clouds, Lysistrata*. London: Penguin, 2002.

Aristotle, *The Complete Works of Aristotle*. Princeton, NJ: Princeton University Press, 1984.

Assad, Maria L. *Reading with Michel Serres: An Encounter with Time*. New York: State University of New York Press, 1999.

Audi, Robert. *Epistemology: A Contemporary Introduction to the Theory of Knowledge*. London: Routledge, 1998.

Bachelard, Gaston. *The Poetics of Space*. New York: Beacon Press, 1992.

Bakhtin, M.M. *Dialogic Imagination: Four Essays*. Austin, TX: University of Texas Press, 1982.

Balcombe, Jonathan. *Pleasurable Kingdom: Animals and the Nature of Feeling Good*. London: Palgrave Macmillan, 2007.

Barasch, Moshe. *Theories of Art*. London: Routledge, 2000.

Barber, Elizabeth Wayland, and Paul T. Barber. *When They*

Severed Earth from Sky: How the Human Mind Shapes Myth.
Princeton, NJ: Princeton University Press, 2006.

Barber, Richard. *The Holy Grail: A Study in Imagination and Belief*. Cambridge, MA: Harvard University Press, 2004.

Bendall, Cecil, and W.H.D. Rouse. *Siksa Samuccaya*. New Delhi: Motilal Banarsidass, 2000.

Benjamin, Walter. *Selected Writings: 1935-1938 v. 3*. Cambridge, MA: Harvard University Press, 2006.

Benjamin, Walter. *Selected Writings: 1927-1934 v. 2*. Cambridge, MA: Harvard University Press, 1999.

Berlin, Isaiah. *The Hedgehog And The Fox: Essay on Tolstoy's View of History*. London: Phoenix, 1999.

Blanchot, Maurice. *Blanchot Reader: Essays and Fiction*. Barrytown, NY: Station Hill Press, 1996.

Bruner, Jerome. *Making Stories: Law, Literature, Life*. Cambridge, MA: Harvard University Press, 2003.

Buckingham, Will. *Levinas, Storytelling and Anti-Storytelling*. London: Bloomsbury, 2013.

Buckingham, Will. *Stealing With the Eyes: Imaginings and Incantations in Indonesia*. London: Haus Publishing, 2018.

Calasso, Roberto. *The Marriage of Cadmus and Harmony*. London: Vintage, 1994.

Calasso, Roberto. *Ka*. London: Vintage, 1999.

Calvino, Italo. *Six Memos for the Next Millennium*. London: Vintage, 1996.

Calvino, Italo. *Invisible Cities*. London: Vintage, 1997.

Calvino, Italo. *If on a Winter's Night a Traveller*. London: Vintage, 1997.

Camille, Michael. *The Gothic Idol: Ideology and Image-Making in Medieval Art*. Cambridge: Cambridge University Press, 1991.

Carnap, Rudolf, and Martin Gardner. *An Introduction to the Philosophy of Science*. Mineola, NY: Dover Publications, 1995.

Caygill, Howard. *Walter Benjamin: The Colour of Experience*. London: Routledge, 1997.

Chanter, Tina. *Time, Death and the Feminine: Levinas with Heidegger.* Redwood City, CA: Stanford University Press, 2002.

Chatwin, Bruce. *The Songlines.* London: Picador, 1998.

Cleary, Thomas F. *Rational Zen: The Mind of Dogen Zenji.* Boulder, CO: Shambhala, 1992.

Cowell, E. B. *The Jataka or Stories of the Buddha's Former Births, volume III-IV.* New Delhi: Motilal Banarsidass, 1990.

Critchley, Simon. "Il y a—Holding Levinas's hand to Blanchot's fire." *In Maurice Blanchot: the Demand of Writing,* edited by Carolyn Bailey Gill, 108-22. London: Routledge, 1996 .

Curtius, Ernst Robert. *European Literature and the Latin Middle Ages.* Princeton, NJ: Princeton University Press, 1991.

Deleuze, Gilles, and Felix Guattari. *A Thousand Plateaus.* London: Continuum, 2001.

Dennett, Daniel C. *Consciousness Explained.* Baltimore, MD: Lippincott Williams and Wilkins, 1992.

Derrida, Jacques. *Writing and Difference.* Chicago: Chicago University Press, 1990.

Derrida, Jacques. *The Gift of Death.* Chicago: Chicago University Press, 1996.

Edie, James M. *Edmund Husserl's Phenomenology.* Bloomington, IN: Indiana University Press, 1997.

Everett, Daniel. *Don't Sleep, There Are Snakes.* London: Profile Books, 2008.

Garfield, Jay L. *The Fundamental Wisdom of the Middle Way: Nagarjuna's Mulamadhyamakakarika.* Oxford: Oxford University Press, 1995.

Garfield, Jay L. *Empty Words: Buddhist Philosophy and Cross-cultural Interpretation.* Oxford University Press, 2001.

Gentilucci, Maurizio, and Michael Corballis. "The Hominid That Talked." In *What Makes Us Human?,* edited by Charles Pasternak, 49-70. Oxford: Oneworld, 2007.

Gibbs, Robert. *Correlations in Rosenzweig and Levinas.* Princeton, NJ: Princeton University Press, 1994.

Gibbs, Robert. *Why Ethics?: Signs of Responsibilities*. Princeton, NJ: Princeton University Press, 2000.

Ginsberg, Allen. *Indian Journals, March 1962-May 1963: Notebooks, Diary, Blank Pages, Writings*. New York: Grove Press, 1996.

Gombrich, Richard. *How Buddhism Began*. London: Continuum, 1996.

Hall, Amy Laura. *Kierkegaard and the Treachery of Love*. Cambridge: Cambridge University Press, 2002.

Hegel, Georg Wilhelm Friedrich. *Phenomenology of Spirit*. Oxford: Oxford University Press, 1979.

Hegel, Georg Wilhelm Friedrich_. *Lectures on the History of Philosophy : Medieval and modern philosophy*. Lincoln, NE: University of Nebraska Press, 1995.

Heidegger, Martin. *Being and Time*. Oxford: Blackwell Publishing, 1978.

Heidegger, Martin. *Basic Writings*. London: Routledge, 1993.

Hoban, Russell. *Riddley Walker*. London: Bloomsbury, 2002.

Hofstadter, Douglas R. *I Am a Strange Loop*. New York: Basic Books, 2008.

Husserl, Edmund. *The Crisis of European Sciences and Transcendental Phenomenology*. Evanston, IL: Northwestern University Press, 1970.

Husserl, Edmund. *Cartesian Meditations: An Introduction to Phenomenology*. Dordrecht: Kluwer Academic Publishers, 1977.

Husserl, Edmund. *Shorter Works*. Notre Dame, IN: University of Notre Dame Press, 1982.

Irigaray, Luce. "The Fecundity of the Caress." *In Face to Face with Levinas*, edited by Richard A. Cohen, 231-56. State University of New York Press, 1986.

Irwin, Robert. *"Arabian Nights": A Companion*. London: Penguin, 1995.

James, William. *Pragmatism: A New Name for Some Old Ways of Thinking*. Indianapolis, IN: Hackett Publishing Co., 1980.

Jay, Martin. "The Actuality of Walter Benjamin." *In Experience*

Without a Subject: Walter Benjamin and the Novel, edited by Laura Marcus and Lynda Nead, 94-102. London: Lawrence & Wishart, 1998.

Jullien, François. *In Praise of Blandness: Proceeding from Chinese Thought and Aesthetics.* Cambridge, MA: Zone Books, 2007.

Kant, Immanuel. *Ethical Philosophy: The Complete Texts of "Grounding for the Metaphysics of Morals" and "Metaphysical Principles of Virtue".* Indianapolis, IN: Hackett Publishing Co., 1995.

Kant, Immanuel. *Critique of Pure Reason.* Cambridge: Cambridge University Press, 1999.

Katz, Claire. *Levinas, Judaism and the Feminine: The Silent Footsteps of Rebecca.* Bloomington, IN: Indiana University Press, 2004.

Khoroche, Peter, and Wendy Doniger. *Once the Buddha was a Monkey: Jatakamala.* University of Chicago Press, 1989.

Kierkegaard, Soren. *Purity of Heart Is to Will One Thing.* London: HarperTorch, 1948.

Kierkegaard, Soren. *Fear and Trembling: Dialectical Lyric* by Johannes De Silentio. London: Penguin Classics, 1985.

Kim, Hee-Jin, and Taigen Dan Leighton. *Eihei Dogen.* Somerville, MA: Wisdom Publications, 2004.

Kolakowski, Leszek. *Husserl and the Search for Certitude.* Chicago: University of Chicago Press, 1987.

Kopf, Gereon. *Beyond Personal Identity.* London: Routledge, 2001.

Lakoff, George, and Mark Johnson. *Philosophy in the Flesh: The Embodied Mind and Its Challenge to Western Thought.* New York: Basic Books, 1999.

Lamont, Peter. *The Rise of the Indian Rope Trick: How a Spectacular Hoax Became History.* London: Abacus, 2005.

Lamotte, Étienne. "Textual Interpretation in Buddhism." In *Buddhist Hermeneutics*, edited by Donald S. Lopez Jr., 11-28. New Delhi: Motilal Banarsidass, 1993.

Levinas, Emmanuel. *Totality and Infinity*. Pittsburgh, PA: Duquesne University Press, 1969.

Levinas, Emmanuel. *Otherwise Than Being, Or, Beyond Essence*. Pittsburgh, PA: Duquesne University Press, 1981.

Levinas, Emmanuel. *Ethics and Infinity: Conversations with Philippe Nemo. Pittsburgh, PA:* Duquesne University Press, 1985.

Levinas, Emmanuel. *Time and the Other.* Duquesne University Press, 1987.

Levinas, Emmanuel *Basic Philosophical Writings*. Bloomington, IN: Indiana University Press, 1996.

Levinas, Emmanuel.*Collected Philosophical Papers*. Pittsburgh, PA: Duquesne University Press, 1998a.

Levinas, Emmanuel. *Of God Who Comes to Mind*. Redwood City, CA: Stanford University Press, 1998b.

Levinas, Emmanuel. *Existence and Existents.* Pittsburgh, PA: Duquesne University Press, 2001a.

Levinas, Emmanuel. *God, Death and Time*. Redwood City, CA: Stanford University Press, 2001b.

Libet, Benjamin. *Mind Time: The Temporal Factor in Consciousness.* Cambridge, MA: Harvard University Press, 2004.

Liu, JeeLoo. *An Introduction to Chinese Philosophy*. Oxford: Blackwell Publishing, 2006.

Llewelyn, John. *Emmanuel Levinas: Genealogy of Ethics*. London: Routledge, 1995.

MacDonald, Michael J. "Losing Spirit: Hegel, Levinas, and the Limits of Narrative." *Narrative* 13, 2 (2005): 182—93.

MacIntyre, Alasdair. *After Virtue.* Oxford: Duckworth, 1997.

Mack, Arien and Irvin Rock. *Inattentional Blindness.* Cambridge, MA: MIT Press, 1998.

Manguel, Alberto. *A History of Reading*. London: Viking/Allen Lane, 1996.

May, Reinhard. *Heidegger's Hidden Sources: East Asian Influences on His Work.* London: Routledge, 1996.

McCaughrean, Geraldine. *100 World Myths and Legends.*

London: Orion Children's, 2001.

McGhee, Michael. *Transformations of Mind: Philosophy as Spiritual Practice*. Cambridge: Cambridge University Press, 2000.

McKinnon, Susan. *From a Shattered Sun: Hierarchy, Gender and Alliance in the Tanimbar Islands*. University of Wisconsin Press, 1992.

Mendes-Flohr, Paul. *Philosophy of Franz Rosenzweig*. University Press of New England, 2006.

Moran, Dermot. *Introduction to Phenomenology*. London: Routledge, 1999.

Nagao, Gadjin. *Madhyamika and Yogacara: Study of Mahayana Philosophies*. State University of New York Press, 1991.

Narayan, R.K. *Gods, Demons and Others*. Minerva, 1994.

Neate, Patrick. *Twelve Bar Blues*. London: Penguin, 2002.

Nietzsche, Friedrich. *The Will to Power: In Science, Nature, Society and Art*. London: Random House, 1973.

Nietzsche, Friedrich. *The Birth of Tragedy: Out of the Spirit of Music*. London: Penguin Classics, 1993.

Niles, John D. *Homo Narrans: The Poetics and Anthropology of Oral Literature*. University of Pennsylvania Press, 1999.

Nussbaum, Martha Craven, and Amélie Rorty. *Essays on Aristotle's De Anima: its agenda and its recent interpreters*. Oxford: Oxford University Press, 1992.

O'Flaherty, Wendy Doniger. *Dreams, Illusions and Other Realities*. Chicago: University of Chicago Press, 1986.

O'Flaherty, Wendy Doniger. *Other People's Myths: The Cave of Echoes*. Macmillan USA, 1990.

Ong, Walter J. *Orality and Literacy*. London: Routledge, 2002.

Parkes, Graham. *Heidegger and Asian Thought*. Hawai'i: University of Hawai'i Press, 1987.

Paul Ricoeur, 20-33. "Life in Quest of Narrative." In *On Paul Ricoeur: Narrative and Interpretation*, edited by David Wood, 20-33. Routledge, 1991.

Paulson, William. "Swimming the Channel." In *Mapping Michel*

Serres, edited by Niran Abbas, 24-36. University of Michigan Press, 2005.

Pitkin, Annabella. "Scandalous Ethics; Infinite Presence with Suffering." In *Between Ourselves: second-person issues in the study of consciousness*, edited by Evan Thompson, 231-46. Exeter: Imprint Academic, 2001.

Plato. *Complete Works*. Hackett Publishing Co, Inc, 1997.

Putnam, Hilary. "Levinas and Judaism." In *The Cambridge Companion to Levinas*, edited by Simon Critchley, and Robert Bernasconi, 33-62. Cambridge: Cambridge University Press, 2002.

Ramanujan, A. K. *The Collected Essays of A.K.Ramanujan*. New Delhi: OUP India, 1998.

Ricoeur, Paul. *Time and Narrative: v. 1*. Chicago: University of Chicago Press, 1990.

Ricoeur, Paul. *Oneself as Another*. Chicago: University of Chicago Press, 1994.

Rosenzweig, Franz. *The Star of Redemption*. Notre Dame, IN: University of Notre Dame Press, 1985.

Rosenzweig, Franz. *The New Thinking*. Syracuse University Press, 1998.

Rushdie, Salman. *Haroun and the Sea of Stories*. London: Granta, 1990.

Sandford, Stella. *The Metaphysics of Love: Gender and Transcendence in Levinas*. London: Continuum, 2000.

Serres, Michel. *Genesis*. University of Michigan Press, 1995.

Serres, Michel. *The Troubadour of Knowledge*. University of Michigan Press, 1997.

Serres, Michel. *The Birth of Physics*. Clinamen Press Ltd, 2000.

Shantideva, trans. Kate Crosby, and Andrew Skilton. *The Bodhicaryavatara*. Oxford: Oxford University Press, 1998.

Simons, D. J. and Chabris, C. F. "Gorillas in our midst: Sustained inattentional blindness for dynamic events." *Perception 28* (1999): 1059—74.

Simons, Daniel J. *Change Blindness and Visual Memory: A Special Issue of Visual Cognition*. Hove: Psychology Press, 2000.

Sissa, Guilia, and Marcel Detienne. *The Daily Life of the Greek Gods*. Redwood City, CA: Stanford University Press, 2000.

Solnit, Rebecca. *Wanderlust: A History of Walking*. London: Viking, 2000.

Somadeva. *Tales from the Kathasaritsagara*. London: Penguin, 1996.

Stafford, William. *Traveling Through the Dark: Poems*. Birmingham: Weatherlight Press, 1997.

Sterne, Laurence. *The Life and Opinions of Tristram Shandy, Gentleman*. London: Penguin Classics, 2003.

Strawson, Galen. "Against Narrativity." *Ratio* 17 (2004): 428—52.

Ströker, Elisabeth. 1997. *Husserlian Foundations of Science*. New York: Springer.

Tamara Wright, Alison Ainley, Peter Hughes. "The Paradox of Morality: an Interview with Emmanuel Levinas." In *The Provocation of Levinas: Rethinking the Other*, edited by Robert Bernasconi, and David Wood, 168-80. London: Routledge, 1988.

Turner, Mark. *The Literary Mind*. Oxford: Oxford University Press, 1998.

Varela, Francisco J, and Evan Thompson. *The Embodied Mind: Cognitive Science and Human Experience*. Cambridge, MA: MIT Press, 1993.

Vasari, Giorgio. *Lives of the Artists*. London: Penguin, 1987.Warner, Marina. *Fantastic Metamorphoses, Other Worlds: Ways of Telling the Self*. Oxford: Oxford University Press, 2004.

Wegner, Daniel M. *The Illusion of Conscious Will*. Cambridge, MA: MIT Press, 2002.

Zimmer, Heinrich Robert, and Joseph Campbell. *Philosophies of India*. Princeton, NJ: Princeton University Press, 1969.

Žižek, Slavoj. *Abyss of Freedom*. University of Ann Arbor, MI: Michigan Press, 1997.

ABOUT THE AUTHOR

Will Buckingham is a freelance writer and philosopher. He has a PhD in philosophy and an MA in social anthropology. He was previously Associate Professor of Writing and Creativity at De Montfort University in the UK. He has taught at universities in the UK, China and elsewhere: most recently as Visiting Professor of Humanities at the Parami Institute, Yangon, Myanmar.

Will writes philosophy, fiction and for children. His books include *Stealing With the Eyes: Imaginings and Incantations in Indonesia* (Haus Publishing, 2018), *Lucy and the Rocket Dog* (Knopf, 2017) and *Levinas, Storytelling and Anti-Storytelling* (Bloomsbury, 2013). He is also a contributor to Dorling Kindersley's global bestseller *The Philosophy Book*.

Will can be found online at www.willbuckingham.com.

ALSO BY WILL BUCKINGHAM

Non-Fiction

Stealing With the Eyes: Imaginings and Incantations in Indonesia. Haus Publishing, 2018.

A Practical Guide to Happiness: Think Deeply and Flourish. Icon Books, 2012 & 2017.

Teach Yourself: Complete Write a Novel. John Murray, 2014.

Levinas, Storytelling and Anti-Storytelling. Bloomsbury, 2013.

Fiction

Lucy and the Rocket Dog. Knopf, 2017.

Sixty-Four Chance Pieces: A Book of Changes. Earnshaw Books, 2015.

Goat Music. Roman Books, 2015.

The Descent of the Lyre. Roman Books, 2012.

The Snorgh and the Sailor. Alison Green Books / Scholastic, 2012.

Cargo Fever. Tindal Street Press, 2008.

Lightning Source UK Ltd.
Milton Keynes UK
UKHW011018110122
396961UK00001B/218